THE USA
1918–1968

John A. Kerr

HODDER
GIBSON
AN HACHETTE UK COMPANY

The Publishers would like to thank the following for permission to reproduce copyright material:

Photo credits: p.1 © Universal Images Group North America LLC/Alamy Stock Photo; **p.2** (top) © Tim Mainiero/Alamy Stock Photo; (bottom) © Aloysius Patrimonio/123RF.com; **p.5** © Claire Spinks/Hodder Gibson; **p.7** © SuperStock ; **p.8** © Everett Collection Historical/Alamy Stock Photo; **p.9** © World History Archive/Alamy Stock Photo; **p.11** © Bettmann/Getty Images; **p.16** © *The Kourier*, July 1934; **p.18** © Friedmann, Leo/The Illinois Publishing Co. (Jacksonville, IL); **p.20** © MPI/Archive Photos/Getty Images; **p.31** via https://rexwarner11.wordpress.com/photos/ accessed 25-04-16; **p.33** © World History Archive/Alamy Stock Photo; **p.34** © GL Archive/Alamy Stock Photo; **p.35** © Lawrence Beitler/Hulton Archive/Getty Images; **p.36** (bottom) *The Great Migration: Journey to the North* by Eloise Greenfield, illustrated by Jan Spivey Gilchrist © HarperCollins Children's Books; **p.37** ©Arthur Siegel/Anthony Potter Collection/Archive Collection/Getty Images; **p.39** © MPI/Getty Images; **p.41** © Everett Collection Historical/Alamy *Stock Photo*; **p.43** © World History Archive/Alamy *Stock Photo*; **p.46** © Mim Friday/Alamy *Stock Photo*; **p.52** montage (left) © Transcendental Graphics/Archive Photos/Getty Images; (top right) © Bettmann/Getty Images; (bottom right) © Ioulia Bolchakova/123rf; **p.54** courtesy The York County Heritage Trust, Pennsylvania; **p.55** via http://www.slideshare.net/LOAPUSH/loapush-ch-32 accessed 25-04-16; **p.57** © The Advertising Archives; **p.58** © Granger, NYC. /Alamy Stock Photo; **p.66** © Lordprice Collection/photographersdirect; **p.67** ©Fotosearch/Archive Photos/Getty Images; **p.68** © IanDagnall Computing/Alamy Stock Photo; **p.74** © IanDagnall Computing/Alamy Stock Photo; **p.75** ©The Granger Collection/Topfoto; **p.76** courtesy of the Franklin D. Roosevelt Library; **p.77** courtesy of *The Houston Post*, October 1933; **p.78** ©Underwood Archives/Archive Photos/Getty Images; **p.80** ©The Granger Collection/Topfoto; **p.81** © MPI/Archive Photos/Getty Images; **p.82** © Boo-hoo the New Deal is ruining the Country', cartoon of the effects of Franklin Roosevelt's (1882-1945) economic policies, 1936 (litho), American School, (20th century)/Private Collection /Peter Newark American Pictures/Bridgeman Images; **p.89** ©The Granger Collection/Topfoto; **p.95** ©Fax, Elton C./NAACP/Library of Congress; **p.97** courtesy *The Advocate* (Baton Rouge, Louisiana), 18 May 1954; **p.98** montage (left) ©Bettmann/Getty Images; (top and bottom right) © The San Antonio Express-News/ZUMA Licensing; **p.99** storyboard montage (top left) © George Marks/Retrofile RF/GettyImages; (top right) © Visions of America, LLC/Alamy Stock Photo; (mid-left) © Clark Brennan/Alamy Stock Photo; (mid-right) © World History Archive/Alamy Stock Photo; (bottom left) © Everett Collection Historical/Alamy Stock Photo; (bottom right) © nsf/Alamy Stock Photo; **p.101** hand-drawn flyer courtesy Jackson Non-violent Movement; **p.103** Reprinted with the permission of Aladdin, an imprint of Simon & Schuster Children's Publishing Division, *from LITTLE ROCK NINE* by Marshall Poe & illustrated by Ellen Lindner. Copyright © 2008 by Ellen Lindner. All rights reserved.; **p.104** *The Manchester Union Leader*, September 26, 1957, courtesy of the University of Arkansas – Special Collections; **p.106** © Everett Collection Historical/Alamy Stock Photo; **p.107** © Everett Collection Historical/Alamy Stock Photo; **p.111** (top) ©BILL HUDSON /AP/Press Association Images; (bottom) © Black Star/Alamy *Stock Photo*; **p.113** (top) © *Tony* Savino/Corbis; (bottom) courtesy of National Action Network; **p.116** ©Flip Schulke/Corbis; **p.117** © Everett Collection Historical/Alamy Stock Photo; **p.124** © Steve Schapiro/Corbis; **p.126** ©Margaret Bourke-White/Time & Life Pictures/Masters/Getty Images; **p127** © Bentley Archive/Popperfoto/Getty Images; **p.129** © *Ed Ford/Library of Congress*; **p.132** ©Bettmann /*Getty images*; **p.134** ©AP/Press Association Images; **p.136** © INTERFOTO/Alamy *Stock Photo*; **p.137** ©AP/Press Association Images; **p.138** ©Bettmann/ Getty Images; **p.140** © Imagestate Media (John Foxx)/ Vol 09 Lifestyles Today

Image used in sidebar panels throughout ©Vepar5/iStock/Thinkstock

Acknowledgements: p.94 – lyrics from *Black, Brown and White* by Big Bill Broonzy © W. Broonzy/ Warner/Chappell Music, Inc. used by kind permission.

Orders: please contact Bookpoint Ltd, 130 Milton Park, Abingdon, Oxon OX14 4SB. Telephone: (44) 01235 827720. Fax: (44) 01235 400454. Lines are open 9.00–5.00, Monday to Saturday, with a 24-hour message answering service. Visit our website at www.hoddereducation.co.uk. Hodder Gibson can be contacted direct on: email: hoddergibson@hodder.co.uk

© John A. Kerr 2016

First published in 2016 by
Hodder Gibson, an imprint of Hodder Education,
An Hachette UK Company
2a Christie Street
Paisley PA1 1NB

Impression number 5 4 3 2 1
Year   2020 2019 2018 2017 2016

Cover photo: United States flag © ptyszku – Fotolia; Monument Valley © Getty Images/iStockphoto/Thinkstock
Illustrations by Aptara, Inc.
Typeset by Aptara, Inc.

Printed in Slovenia

A catalogue record for this title is available from the British Library
ISBN: 978 14718 5249 7

Contents

Introduction

What is in this book?

This book is about the USA between 1918 and 1968.

In 1900 the USA was still a young country but it was growing fast. It had huge resources and attracted millions of people from around the world looking for a new life and the opportunity to be free and become rich.

However, there were underlying tensions within the USA that were to cause problems between 1918 and 1968. These tensions run throughout all seven chapters of this book, in some more strongly than others.

This book will explore three main areas of tension in the USA:

- tension between the national government of the USA, known as Federal Authority, and the rights of individual states, called States' Rights;
- tensions in the economy between the rich, who wanted to become richer without any government control, and those who thought the government should take more control over the economy to make a fairer society for everyone;
- tensions between racial groups in the USA.

How will this book help you?

This book will help you to be successful in your Higher History course. It contains everything you need to know about the unit called 'USA, 1918–68'.

The book provides advice and examples to help you be successful with Higher examinations and unit assessments. All unit assessment tasks should be carried out under the supervision and control of assessors. The aim of unit assessment is to gather evidence of learners' skills at each level. Therefore, learners can have access to their materials and notes during unit assessment. The time taken to complete the unit assessment should be negotiated with learners, based on their needs. This book offers several examples of approaches to unit assessment. The book also contains questions at the end of each chapter duplicating the style of Higher extended response questions.

The activities

At the end of each chapter there is an activity section divided into three broad categories:

Category 1

In category 1 there are tasks to focus on knowledge and understanding of the chapter content. The first of these is called 'If this is the answer, what is the question?' This is useful to focus on the main facts of the chapter. However, rather than asking direct questions this task requires students to identify the information and formulate a question that is unambiguous but is structured in such a way as can only result in the answer provided. To achieve that target students must understand the context of the answer.

The second task is called 'How far can you go?' The questions are set in pairs. The first two test basic information recall and understanding while the others encourage higher levels of learning outcome.

Category 2

Category 2 activities provide models of activities, often within a group context that provide a variety of approaches to learning. These activities are not 'locked' into a particular topic but provide a teacher resource that can be adapted to suit other sections in this book or indeed other topics generally.

Category 3

Category 3 provides examples of questions as they could appear in Section 3: Europe and the World, of the final exam. The questions can also be used as titles for the Assignment. There are also examples of unit assessment questions.

1 Background: the USA in 1918

The flag

In 1918 the flag of the USA had 13 red and white stripes and 48 white stars on a blue background.

The 48 stars on a blue background represented the 48 individual states that made up the United States. The 13 red and white stripes represented the 13 original states that had declared their independence from Britain in 1776. Between 1776 and 1918 the USA grew into a country of 48 states.

> **Source 1.1**
>
> **The flag of the USA in 1918.**
>
> **Why does this flag only have 48 stars when the present US flag has 50? What must have happened to the USA between 1918 and now to cause the change?**
>
>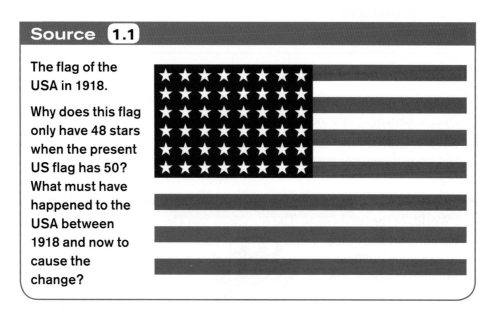

What is the USA?

In 1918 the USA had 48 states. The national government was called the federal government and passed laws in Congress which affected the whole nation.

Each state also had its own government which made laws which applied only to that individual state. Each state guarded its States' Rights against any threat from the federal government to take away its independence.

Source 1.2

The seal of the Federal Judiciary of the USA.

The Federal Judiciary of the United States is one of the three branches of the federal government of the United States. Its motto is *E pluribus unum*. Find out what that means and how it links to the chapter on immigration.

The government of the USA

The USA is a republic, which means that there is no royal family – no King or Queen. Instead, at the head of government is the President, elected every four years. In 1918 the President was Woodrow Wilson and there were two main national political parties – Democrats and Republicans.

Source 1.3

This cartoon illustrates the two main political parties in the USA: the Democrats and the Republicans.

Find out why the cartoon shows an elephant and a donkey and why the words GOP and DEMOS feature on their hats.

The USA has a written Constitution which gives rights to each US citizen.

Any new law must not infringe or damage the rights of any individual as guaranteed by the constitution. These rights are called constitutional rights.

All national laws are made in Congress, which meets in the Capitol building in Washington DC. Congress is comprised of two parts: the House of Representatives and the Senate.

Voters in each state of the USA elect representatives who meet in the House of Representatives and senators who meet in the Senate. Each representative represents roughly the same number of voters so the number of representatives from each state varies depending on the population size of the state.

The Senate contains two senators from each state regardless of the population size of the state.

The population of the USA

In 1918 the USA was growing fast. In 1850 there had been only 23 million people and just 30 per cent of these lived in towns with more than 2500 people. Between 1901 and 1920, the population of the United States grew to over 105 million with half of all Americans living in towns and cities. During this time, almost 15 million 'new' immigrants came to America.

The huge rise in population was caused by immigration. Millions of people left their homelands and came to America looking for a new life. By 1920, 42 per cent of New Yorkers, 41 per cent of Chicagoans and 42 per cent of San Franciscans were foreign-born. Immigrants, many speaking little or no English, tended to cluster in areas where other immigrants who shared the same culture had already settled. As a result, areas of cities came to be known as Little Italy or Little Poland because of the people who settled there.

The USA in the world

The USA joined the First World War in 1917 and was a main reason why Germany was defeated. In 1918 the USA was one of the big three world powers that won the First World War.

The USA had also helped other countries pay for the war by lending them money. By 1918 the USA was the world's biggest creditor nation. That meant the USA was owed billions of dollars by other countries who had borrowed money from the USA. In the 1920s the USA loaned huge amounts to Europe, especially Germany, to create political and economic stability and prosperity in post-war countries. However, when the financial collapse happened in 1929 and America wanted its money back fast, Europe suffered the consequences. One of those consequences was the rise of the Nazis under Adolf Hitler and there are some historians who argue that the Second World War was a direct result of American economic collapse in 1929.

Tensions and problems in the USA

WASPs v new immigrants

WASPs was a nickname given to families that had lived in America for a long time. The letters W A S P stand for White Anglo-Saxon Protestant. The parents and grandparents of established Americans had come from Britain, Germany and Scandinavia. However, by the end of the nineteenth century not only were the numbers of immigrants swelling but the countries from which they came were also changing. Unlike earlier immigrants, the majority of the newcomers after 1900 came from southern, central and eastern Europe especially Italy, Poland and Russia, which were countries quite different in culture and language from the United States. Despite the established Americans being related to immigrants themselves, those 'native' Americans disliked the new immigrants who arrived from central and southern Europe because the new immigrants had different languages, customs and religions and threatened the WASP idea of what America should be like.

Rugged individualism v federal intervention

It was widely believed that the USA was created by tough individuals who took risks to open up America. These tough individuals were the creators of the belief in rugged individualism. Americans in 1900 argued that since their parents and grandparents had fought and struggled to tame the wilderness of North America without any help from the government then why should people look for help from the government now? The supporters of rugged individualism believed that people and businesses should be free to work hard and make money any way they could without interference from the government.

On the other side of the argument, supporters of federal intervention wanted central government to get involved (intervene) in influencing and controlling businesses and working conditions in order to help the weak and poor.

Source 1.4

'Rely on yourself NOT the government!'

What important political ideas are contained within the slogan on this mug? Why have you decided that?

RELY ON
YOURSELF
NOT
THE
GOVERNMENT!

Black v white

Slavery had ended in 1865 but in the Southern states a system of segregation and discrimination continued to make life hard and dangerous for black Americans. When black Americans moved north looking for a better life they found discrimination and segregation also existed in the Northern cities.

World power v isolationist

The USA had become the strongest and richest country in the world by 1918 but many Americans wanted nothing to do with the outside world. Millions of immigrants had risked everything to leave Europe behind them. Why should they want to get involved in Europe's problems again? Isolationists wanted to isolate themselves politically from Europe or Asia, although it soon became clear that the economies of Europe and the USA were closely linked.

Immigration and the USA – changing attitudes 2

The focus of this chapter is immigration to America at the beginning of the twentieth century.

During the nineteenth century America had grown from a relatively unexplored continent into an economic giant. After 1880 America entered a period of fast economic growth and needed increasing numbers of workers to fill the growing number of factory jobs. At the end of 1918, the USA was the world's wealthiest nation. Demand created its own supply. Millions of Europeans, unable to bear the pressures of unemployment, depressions and famine, looked towards America as a land of plenty, a land of opportunity and a place where they could achieve the 'American Dream'.

For many Americans the 'American Dream' means the opportunity for anyone, regardless of their background, to become successful if they work hard. The American Dream also means equality of opportunity and the chance 'to make good'. All immigrants came to America hoping to find a better life where they would be free and happy. Thousands of immigrants flocked to the nation in the 'pursuit of happiness'.

Why was the USA such a magnet for immigrants?

Between 1900 and 1915, more than 15 million immigrants arrived in the United States. That was about equal to the number of immigrants who had arrived in the previous 40 years. In 1910, three-quarters of New York City's population were either immigrants or first-generation Americans (the sons and daughters of immigrants).

Source 2.1

'America' greeting immigrants at a gate.

Describe as many features as possible in this cartoon which relate to immigration to the USA and the American Dream around 1920. You should be able to comment on at least eight notable points.

Push and pull

People usually decide to move to another country because of 'push' or 'pull' reasons or a combination of both. Push reasons are factors that force people to move because they want to get away from things that make life hard or dangerous. For migrants leaving Europe, push reasons included escaping religious, racial and political persecution; land and job shortages; rising taxes; or leaving behind crop failures and starvation.

Pull reasons were things that attracted people to go to the USA. For example, people went to the USA because it was thought of as the land of economic opportunity where jobs were easy to get and where, by working hard, everyone could achieve the American Dream.

The 'new' immigrants made the journey to America for the same reasons as the earlier immigrants from northern and western Europe. Although immigrants often settled near the ports where they arrived in the USA, a large number did find their way inland, attracted by many states that advertised jobs or land for farming. Railroad companies advertised the availability of free or cheap farmland in pamphlets distributed overseas in many languages, bringing agricultural workers to the Midwest farmlands.

Meanwhile in the industrialised Northeast of the USA, coal mines and steel mills soaked up Hungarians, Poles, Slovaks and Italians, while textile mills attracted Greeks. Street trading from barrows and the tailoring trades were popular activities for Russian and Polish Jews.

In summary, the vast majority of immigrants crowded into the growing cities, searching for their chance to make a better life for themselves.

Source 2.2

Why does the Statue of Liberty remain such an iconic symbol for so many people around the world even today?

The USA was like a magnet of hope and for most immigrants the first thing they saw as they approached New York was the Statue of Liberty, completed in 1886. The Statue holds high a torch, symbolising liberty (freedom) and the hope for a brighter future. The poem at the base of the statue sums up the reasons why so many immigrants went to America.

Give me your tired, your poor
Your huddled masses yearning to breathe free (yearning = wanting)
The wretched refuse of your teeming shore (wretched = poor; refuse = people with no hope; teeming = overcrowded)
Send these, the homeless tempest-tost to me (tempest-tost = caught in a storm and battered)
I lift my lamp beside the golden door! (golden door = entrance to opportunities and wealth in America)

From The New Colossus, *by Emma Lazarus*

The 'Melting Pot'

Until the early twentieth century America had an 'open door' policy for immigrants, meaning that almost anyone could enter the country and as a result by 1918 the USA was a multi-ethnic society. In 1915, President Woodrow Wilson delivered his famous 'melting pot' speech:

> 66 *America is like a huge melting pot. We will mix the races together to create a new person – an American.*

America has always been a land of immigrants. One definition of an American is somebody who came from somewhere else to become someone else. But how true was the ideal of people from all different backgrounds merging together into one united family of Americans?

Until the middle of the nineteenth century, most immigrants came from northern Europe, in particular from Britain, Ireland, Germany and Scandinavia. These 'older' immigrants took pride in how they had defeated the 'Red Indians', opened up the USA and made it a strong country. They said that the resources of the USA were gifts from God to be used to their advantage. They claimed it was their **manifest destiny** to develop the USA and keep it safe for their White Anglo-Saxon Protestant way of life.

Source 2.3

This painting tries to depict the idea of manifest destiny. It shows the early immigrants from northern and western Europe civilising the Wild West. How does it attempt to convey the belief of older immigrants that they had a natural right to take over and develop the USA?

By the end of the nineteenth century the type of immigrant arriving in America was changing. Immigrants from northern and western Europe continued coming as they had for three centuries, but after 1890, more than 80 per cent of arrivals were so-called 'New Immigrants', from southern and eastern Europe. They were seen by WASP Americans as culturally and racially quite different from the Germans, Britons and other northwest Europeans who had made up the bulk of the immigration into the United States in earlier times. After the 1880s, those 'new' immigrants from eastern and southern European countries looked for safety and hope, escaping persecution and economic hardship in their homeland and believing that by working hard they could build new, better lives for themselves in America.

However, recent studies have discovered a different picture of the motives of many younger 'new' immigrants. The most surprising discovery is that they did not intend to stay in the USA. These immigrants, mostly young and male, hoped to earn enough money during a temporary stay in America to be able to afford an increased standard of living upon returning to their homeland. Somewhere between 50 and 80 per cent of the new immigrants are believed to have eventually returned to their countries of origin. Perhaps it was also because of this intention to return home that many new immigrants preferred to stay in 'towns within cities' where ethnic groups created their own communities, with their own banks, cinemas, clubs, shops and religious centres. These Little Italys, Little Polands or Little Greeces provided secure and familiar surroundings to new immigrants but perhaps they also created problems for the newcomers.

By 1900 most power in the USA was in the hands of the 'older' immigrants, nicknamed WASPs. As mentioned earlier, WASP stands for White Anglo-Saxon Protestant. These immigrants, who were descended from northern Europeans, were obviously white, they came originally from a part of northern Europe that is described as Anglo-Saxon and they were mostly Protestant.

'Established Americans' – the WASPS – were very different in background to, and increasingly resentful and suspicious of, the new immigrants. Established Americans also saw the 'towns within cities' as centres of alien cultures filled with people who seemed not to want to be American and therefore worried that these new immigrants might be undermining the American way of life. While it is true that the vast majority of the population of the United States – more than 85 per cent – remained native-born citizens, an especially heavy concentration of immigrants in major cities created the feeling of a foreign takeover. So tension increased between established Americans and new immigrants.

The Dillingham Commission

The US Government wanted to know more about the problem of immigration, especially the 'new immigrants'. Formed in 1907, the

Dillingham Commission discovered that since the 1880s immigrants had mainly come from southern and eastern Europe. The Commission believed that immigrants from places like Russia, Italy, Turkey, Lithuania and Greece were inferior to the WASP-type immigrants arriving before 1890. The Commission recommended that literacy tests be used to make it harder for 'inferior' immigrants to get into the USA. In other words, if an immigrant could not read or write he or she would find it difficult to get into the USA.

When war broke out in Europe in 1914, the flood of immigrants was greatly reduced, but with the end of the war in 1918 the US Government feared that many more millions of immigrants would travel to America to start new lives. At the same time attitudes in America were getting tougher towards immigrants. Many WASP Americans were afraid that the arrival of new immigrants from southern and eastern Europe threatened their way of life. This fear of immigrants who were in some ways different from the 'WASPs' resulted in attacks on immigrants and new laws designed to restrict their entry into America. For the first time the Government of the USA considered closing the open door on immigrants.

Source 2.4

The figure in the red striped trousers is Uncle Sam, a figure that represents the USA. The smaller figure to the right of Uncle Sam is a US politician. The cartoon is about the problem of immigrants arriving in the USA.

Describe and explain as many features as you can in this cartoon that illustrate the belief that there are too many immigrants arriving in the USA and that they cause worry, crime and problems for the USA.

Changing attitudes towards immigrants

In 1917 two writers, Grace Abbott and Julian Mack, explained why attitudes towards immigrants were changing in the USA.

> *Who among those people who want to enter the United States should we stop coming in? This question is prompted by the general distrust of any stranger, by an exaggeration of our own virtues and a minimising of the virtues of others. There are many Americans today who believe that every immigrant is a barbarian, an uncivilised brute. These Americans are led by their prejudices to accept sweeping condemnations to the effect that our political difficulties are due to the immigrants' ignorance and inexperience, that crime and poverty can be traced to him and other evils are predicted for the future.*
>
> From The Immigrant and the Community *by Grace Abbott and Julian W. Mack, 1917*

Americans blamed many of their problems on the new immigrants. In the aftermath of war, tensions increased in America. Unemployment rose and industrial disputes and strikes increased as workers tried to improve their living and working conditions. In this time of tension Americans looked around for something to blame and immigrants were an easy target. US politicians were not slow to jump on the immigration bandwagon. Immigrants had no votes and being strong against immigration was a good vote catcher. As a result of growing public concern US politicians began to campaign for immigration restrictions.

In 1920 the Republican Party announced in their election campaign that, 'the immigration policy of the USA should be to favour immigrants whose standards are similar to ours'. More directly, a senator from Alabama, hoping to be re-elected, said:

> *... as soon as immigrants step off the decks of their ships they become a problem for us. They bring Bolshevism and red anarchy. They take jobs that belong to the good citizens of the USA. They are a danger and a menace to us every day. They must be stopped!*

Why did attitudes change towards immigrants?

The first and most immediate reason why anyone changes their attitudes about anything is when their personal comfort zone is upset, and the waves of new immigrants arriving in the cities of Northeastern USA were certainly upsetting the lives of many ordinary Americans.

Worries about housing

One increasing problem was a shortage of housing at reasonable rent. In the Northeast of the USA, in and around New York, the large numbers of immigrants did make life harder for working-class Americans. Newly arrived immigrants needed somewhere to live and that created higher demand for the available housing supply. Landlords knew that high demand meant they could raise rents without necessarily improving the quality of their housing. As a result the WASP working-class saw their rents being forced up and housing harder to find due to the impact of immigration.

Worries about jobs

Another source of difficulty for many city-based workers was not directly caused by immigration but it was made worse by immigrants. This problem was the competition for unskilled jobs.

In the early 1900s, new ways of working in factories were being introduced that speeded up the production of many things. The production line method broke down production jobs into small automated processes with workers doing smaller, more repetitive jobs alongside a conveyor belt that brought components to them. This new production process meant skilled workers could easily be replaced by unskilled immigrant workers. Factory owners realised they could make huge profits while at the same time employing immigrants on rock bottom wages. Suddenly skilled workers in factories saw their jobs threatened by competition from new immigrants. Of course, it was not the fault of the immigrants but nevertheless dislike of immigrants increased.

At the same time as new working methods in factories reduced the need for skilled workers, American workers became dissatisfied with the rising costs of living, long hours and low wages and tried to band together to form unions in an attempt to protect jobs, increase wages and improve working conditions. In 1919 alone, over four million workers went on strike. However, bosses simply replaced strikers with new immigrant 'strike breakers'. The Italian or Polish or Russian immigrants were known as 'blackleg labour' because they were prepared to work longer hours for lower wages than their American fellow workers. After all, they were still able to earn more than would have been possible back home in the 'old country'.

As the resentment towards immigrant strike breakers and rising rents increased, so did the desire to stop immigrants coming into the country.

Worries about crime

In the early 1920s, crime was increasing and many American politicians chose to blame immigrants. Crime had always existed in America and organised gangs had operated in New York and other cities for a long time. However, the newspapers of the time now had a new word to play with – the Mafia! The Mafia is a name for organised crime gangs who originated

in Sicily, Italy. Naturally, as thousands of Italians emigrated to America, so the Mafia became established in America also.

Newspapers were full of the names of gangsters and the new movies glamorised these gangsters, the most famous being Al 'Scarface' Capone. Although Capone was not a Mafia gangster, the public read an Italian name, and linked it with crime. In the public's imagination it seemed clear that an easy way to stop the increase in crime would be to stop immigration.

However, ironically, a new government law that was meant to make America a calmer and more peaceful place exploded into gang warfare and made organised crime in America even bigger.

The US Government believed that drinking alcohol was a bad thing and in January 1920 the Volstead Act was passed, banning the sale and consumption of alcohol. This was the start of Prohibition – a time when the production and sale of 'booze' was prohibited. Banning alcohol is one thing but it did not stop people wanting to drink alcohol, so the organised crime gangs stepped in to supply the booze themselves. 'Turf wars' broke out between those gangs who wanted to control the supply of illegal alcohol. In the minds of the public, a strong connection was made between crime and the organised gangs of Italian immigrants.

Worries about morality

As newspapers reported more and more tales of gangster gun fights and murders, small town America – away from the cities – thought their way of life was under serious threat from the 'Sinful Cities'. The development of large, thriving communities of immigrants within the cities of the Northeast especially caused a backlash among native-born Americans who feared they were losing their cities to 'undesirable' newcomers. Many Americans lived in small towns and communities that felt under threat. They felt their religious beliefs, their social customs and their democratic political system – in fact their whole way of life – was now under threat from mass immigration. Before the arrival of the 'new' immigrants, more than 60 per cent of the American population could trace their ancestry back to either the British Isles or Germany. These 'established' Americans from northwestern Europe viewed the new arrivals – mostly darker skinned Jews and Catholics from southern and eastern Europe – as not just different but 'inferior'.

Americans who worried that their old small-town American values were under threat were called nativists. Nativists focused their efforts on blocking immigration altogether.

In the prejudiced imagination of many nativist Americans, new immigrants lacked self-discipline and work ethic, lived immoral lifestyles and were often anarchist troublemakers. Before 1921, with one exception (the Chinese Exclusion Act of 1882, immigration into the United States had never been restricted by federal law. That was about to change. To many nativists, the new 'science' of eugenics was very attractive. Supporters of eugenics claimed it was a science that could prove there were such things as superior and inferior racial groups and that the American population could be kept healthy and strong by selective breeding, sterilisation of 'inferior' people and even euthanasia.

'Nativism' was given scientific respectability when Madison Grant published *The Passing of the Great Race*. Grant's book claimed that the world was divided into superior and inferior races. He believed north European immigrants ('Nordics') were far superior to the new type of immigrant and should therefore be encouraged to settle in America. On the other hand, people from southern and eastern Europe were thought to be inferior and should be stopped from emigrating to the USA.

The Immigration Restriction League was the first American organisation associated officially with eugenics. The League wanted to ban what it considered inferior races from entering America. The League felt that social and sexual involvement between 'Americans' and people from less civilised races would pose a biological threat to the American population by weakening the American gene pool. The League wanted literacy tests for immigrants, based on the belief that literacy rates were low among 'inferior' races. Literacy tests for immigrants were started in 1917.

The most famous nativist organisation had recently reinvented itself as *the* white, Protestant social group of the 1920s. It was called the Ku Klux Klan (KKK).

Prejudice, racism and the Ku Klux Klan

The original Ku Klux Klan was organised in the South after the Civil War and it specialised in terrorising black Americans to prevent them from using their newly given civil rights. For reasons linked to the politics of late nineteenth century America, the Klan had withered away by the turn of the century. However, in 1915 the Klan was reinvented and declared itself in support of '100 per cent Americanism'. The new Klan was based on a new anti-immigrant, anti-Catholic and anti-Semitic (against Jews) agenda along with its long hatred of African-Americans. A 1917 publication by the Ku Klux Klan called *The ABC of the Invisible Empire* identified the Klan's goals as 'maintaining white supremacy and protecting ideals of a pure Americanism'.

The revival of the Ku Klux Klan coincided with the release of a film – *The Birth of a Nation*. It was the greatest movie so far in the history of cinema and it controversially showed the Ku Klux Klan as heroes, protecting white women from attack by black robbers and rapists. The film set box office records that stood unbeaten for 22 years and it was the first film ever shown in the White House. The President, Woodrow Wilson, even approved of the new version of Klan history, calling the version of history shown in the movie as, 'all so terribly true'.

Immigration and the USA – changing attitudes

Of course, the image of the Klan in the movie as heroic defenders of an American way of life was nonsense, but white Americans believed it. The film was also significant in that it unintentionally became the inspiration for the 'look' of the Klan that we recognise today. The long white robes with pointed hoods, cross burnings, strange rituals and mysterious language first seen in *The Birth of a Nation* were all turned into reality by the new Klan, which presented itself as a nativist and patriotic organisation.

The film almost single-handedly guaranteed the success of the new Ku Klux Klan, which was started in 1915 by a failed doctor named William J. Simmons. Simmons organised a new Klan in Atlanta, Georgia. He publicised the start of the new Ku Klux Klan by burning a fiery cross on top of Stone Mountain.

Almost immediately support for the Klan spread across the USA. The widespread popularity of the Ku Klux Klan in the 1920s revealed the depth of nativist resistance to the speed of change happening in the USA in the 1920s and the arrival of millions of 'new' immigrants.

The new Klan restricted its membership to native-born white Protestants and campaigned against Catholics, Jews, Communists and immigrants as well as African-Americans. By redefining its enemies, the Klan broadened its appeal to parts of the North and Midwest, and for a time, its membership swelled. WASPs welcomed the Klan into their churches, their homes and their lives.

Source 2.5

'America for Americans'

Why do you think KKK leaders decided that 1915 would be a good time to revive the KKK with its new slogan of '100 per cent Americanism'?

The Klan won almost complete control of the state governments of Colorado and Indiana, and they had big political influence in Oregon, Oklahoma, Tennessee and several other states. An estimated four million Americans were paid members; some historians even claim that President Warren G. Harding had been made a Klan member in a secret ceremony inside the White House.

Membership of the Klan shot up in the early 1920s, largely because of its patriotic, anti-immigrant policies supported by nativists. Although membership of the Klan fell back to around one million by 1929, it remained useful in maintaining WASP control over state politics away from the Northeastern cities.

Worries about revolutionaries and terrorists

So far, the reasons for anti-immigrant attitudes have been based on personal fears and prejudice, but there were also fears about the threats immigrants posed to the American nation. That fear was called the 'Red Scare'.

The event that triggered the greatest national worry about what the millions of new immigrants brought with them was the Bolshevik Revolution of 1917 in Russia. As many thousands of immigrants to the USA came from Russia and eastern Europe, the American authorities began to fear that the immigrants would bring Bolshevik (communist) or anarchist ideas with them and perhaps start a revolution. The use of the word 'anarchist' was used in the USA in much the same way we use 'terrorist' today. The Bolsheviks were known as Reds because the revolutionary flag used in Russia was red.

In 1919, there was a wave of strikes in the USA and many Americans claimed that the strikes were caused by revolutionary immigrants. Americans feared that a small organised group of revolutionaries could seize power in the United States just as they had done in Russia.

In April 1919, the postal service intercepted nearly 40 letter bombs addressed to important US citizens. Wrapped inside the parcels were anarchist leaflets that declared:

 ... there will have to be bloodshed. There will have to be murder, we will kill. There will have to be destruction, we will destroy. We are ready to do anything to destroy the American system.

Whether or not the leaflets really existed did not matter because the US authorities said they did exist and as a result most of the American public were convinced that there was a high risk of revolution. American newspapers were full of reports of how Mitchell Palmer, the top law enforcement officer in America, led raids to arrest suspected terrorists. He even announced that an attempted revolution would start on 1 May 1919. Palmer used the Alien and Sedition Act to arrest and deport 6000 alleged subversives. However, critics pointed out that Palmer had ambitions to stand for the Presidency of the USA and he used the Red Scare to show

himself as a protector of American values. Unfortunately for Palmer, when 1 May came and went with no hint of trouble it became clear that there was no risk of revolution in America. The Red Scare fizzled out and Palmer lost support. However, the Red Scare and the actions of Palmer stuck in the public mind and suspicion of immigrants continued to increase.

Source 2.6

'We'll never change the white and blue to red.'

Describe and explain the content and purpose of this poster and how it represents attitudes in the USA in the early 1920s.

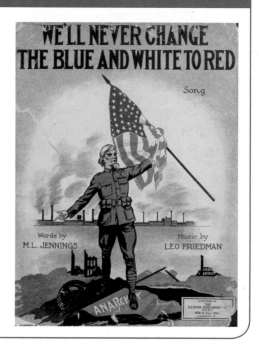

The suspicion of immigrants along with nativist fears of new immigrants, rising crime and political anarchism all reached a head over the case of Sacco and Vanzetti.

Nicola Sacco and Bartolomeo Vanzetti were Italian immigrants who had arrived in the USA in 1908. They made no secret of their support for an anarchist group that supported the use of revolutionary violence, including bombing and assassinations. However, there is NO evidence they were involved in any terrorist activities. On Christmas Eve 1919, an attempted armed robbery took place. It failed and the would-be robbers ran away. Four months later, in April 1920, another robbery took place in the same area. This time the robbers got away with $15,000 in a stolen car, killing two men including the postmaster.

One month later, Sacco and Vanzetti were arrested and accused of armed robbery. When their car was searched the police found radical anti-government leaflets plus handguns. To make things worse, neither Sacco nor Vanzetti could prove where they had been on the day of the murders. From the beginning, public opinion was against them due to their political ideas and because they were immigrants.

To this day many people think the trial of Sacco and Vanzetti was a 'fix' just to show strong government action against immigrants. There was almost no evidence against the two men. The defence had 107 witnesses who swore they had seen the two men somewhere else when the crime was committed. During the court case in May 1921, Judge Webster Thayer was prejudiced against the two men. There was even a man who admitted that he had committed the crime. Despite worldwide support, Sacco and Vanzetti lost their appeal and in August they both died in the electric chair. It was clear that they had simply 'fitted the frame'. Sacco and Vanzetti were not recent immigrants but they were olive skinned, were from Italian families and were anarchists. That meant they wanted to change the political system of America, possibly by violence. Finally, they were linked to 'Italian crime' so they were perfect targets for anti-immigrant prejudice. The case over the two alleged murderers and robbers seemed to display to the world America's paranoia and prejudice. After the trial the judge was overheard boasting, 'Did you see what I did to those dago bastards?' (Dago is an insulting term for an Italian immigrant.)

Worries about the outside world

During the war many Americans resented having to become involved in Europe's problems. After all, most of them had chosen to leave Europe's problems behind when they left for America. After the war the US Government became isolationist. That meant they wanted nothing to do with any problems outside America. For that reason many US citizens did not want fresh waves of immigrants bringing 'European' problems to America.

Another issue concerned the use of propaganda in America during the war. A large part of the US immigrant population was of German or Austrian origin but during the war the American public were persuaded that Germany was an enemy of America. Propaganda stories reported German atrocities during the war. Although some of those stories were made up, the public in America came to resent and dislike immigrants from Germany and the old Austrian empire.

How did America's open door for immigrants close in the 1920s?

For a long time America had been proud of its open door policy, but even before 1900, immigration from China had been stopped. The Chinese Exclusion Act of 1882 was the first important law restricting immigration into the United States. In 1902 Chinese immigration was made illegal, and in 1907 the Japanese Government promised to stop the emigration of its citizens to the USA.

Then in 1917 there was another attempt to limit immigration, especially from the poorer southern and eastern areas of Europe. The 1917 Immigration Act set up a literacy test that required immigrants over 16 years old to pass a basic reading and understanding test in any language. Many of the poorer immigrants, especially those from eastern Europe, had received no education and therefore failed the tests and were refused entry.

However, the literacy test was just the first step in 'closing the door' into the USA. By the end of the 1920s a series of laws had been passed to restrict immigration to the USA. All of the laws showed racial bias since it was still easier for northern Europeans to enter the USA than for those from southern and eastern Europe.

In 1921 the US Government took another step towards closing the open door for immigrants. The Emergency Quota Act of 1921 set up a quota system that only allowed a limited number of immigrants into the country. That number was based on the proportion of people from that country already living in the USA when the census of 1910 was carried out. The law also restricted the total number of immigrants to 357,000 per year.

Every ten years most governments count how many people live in a country. That count is called a census. The US Government knew from its 1910 census how many people of different nationalities lived in the USA. The US Government then announced that only 3 per cent of each nationality already in the United States, according to the 1910 census, would be allowed to come into America.

Source 2.7

Describe exactly what is happening in this cartoon. Then explain in detail how the cartoon links closely to what was happening to the open door to immigration in the USA in the 1920s.

However, the Government soon realised it had underestimated the numbers of new immigrants already in the USA in 1910. By using the 1910 census it was accepting that many thousands of 'new' immigrants could still get into the country. Within three years the Government made it even harder to get into the USA – but only for some people!

The 1924 National Origins Act reduced the quota to 2 per cent and changed the census used to 1890 when there were far fewer 'new' immigrants living in the USA. The new law also completely excluded immigrants from Asia.

Both the 1921 and the 1924 Immigration Acts discriminated unfairly against people who were not from western Europe. Eastern European immigration to the US only increased in the final decades of the nineteenth century, so using the population in 1890 as the basis for the quotas in the new law effectively made mass migration from eastern Europe impossible.

The new laws had a varied effect on immigration numbers. Immigration from Great Britain and Ireland fell 19 per cent, while immigration from Italy fell more than 90 per cent. After the new laws, immigration from southern and eastern Europe was limited to just 22,000 per year – a 97 per cent reduction from pre-restriction levels. Another example is that in the ten years following 1900, about 200,000 Italians arrived in America every year. After the 1924 quota, only 4000 per year were allowed.

By 1929 it became even harder to gain entry to the USA. Only 150,000 immigrants a year were allowed to enter the United States and 85 per cent of all places were reserved for immigrants from northern and western Europe. By 1930, immigration from southern and eastern Europe and Asia had almost entirely stopped.

While the immigration restriction acts of 1921 and 1924 reflected the nativist, anti-immigrant attitudes of many Americans during the 1920s, it is important to note that the laws' practical effects were not as great as expected at the time. Because of difficulties in working out the precise proportions of the 1890 population that belonged to each country, the laws did not take effect until 1929. Within weeks the Wall Street Crash triggered an economic depression in America which made the USA a far less attractive place to go. As a result, the flow of immigration to the USA fell away to a trickle rather than the flood of ten years earlier.

Activities

1 If this is the answer what is the question?

Below you will find a list of words or names. You have to make up a question that can only be answered by the word on the list. For example, if the word 'Immigrant' was the answer, a question could be 'What name was given to people who travelled to America to start a new life?'

Here is your list of answers:

- Federal
- Congress
- WASP
- Nativism
- Red Scare
- American Dream
- Statue of Liberty
- Sacco and Vanzetti
- 100 per cent Americanism
- Quotas

2 How far can you go?

Each set of two questions increases in difficulty. The first two are straightforward describe-and-explain questions. The final few questions require you to think quite hard about the chapter you have read. It is your choice where you stop.

a) Write a list of any pieces of information you can remember about why people migrated to the USA in the early twentieth century.

b) Can you provide a definition for the phrases *laissez faire* and *rugged individualism*?

c) How would you summarise the attitudes of many 'WASPs' to the 'new immigrants' arriving in the USA?

d) What was the underlying theme of the immigration laws passed in the 1920s?

e) If you had access to all US Government resources in 1918, how would you have dealt with the tensions in America at that time?

f) Do you believe that the ideal of the American Melting Pot was ever likely to be achieved?

3 Rewrite

This activity is based on what the senator from Alabama said on page 12 .

continued ➜

a) Rewrite the statement using different words so that it contains the same ideas but is presented in different language. Your version must not add or take away any meaning in the original statement and it cannot use the same words.

b) Design a graphic presentation of the Alabama senator's ideas. Your graphic can be in the style of a graphic novel, a single cartoon, a flowchart or any other format that puts across ideas in a visual style.

Design: Changing attitudes towards immigration

Design a graphic, perhaps a spider diagram, illustrating the reasons why attitudes changed towards immigration in the 1920s. The purpose of doing this is to summarise the relevant section in the chapter.

Your task is to:

- Think of an appropriate heading for each reason and include them in your graphic.

- Find and select one image that you think best illustrates your point.

- Then write a maximum of three sentences explaining why attitudes changed.

Your graphic must make use of colour to enhance learning – for example different coloured headings with colour co-ordinated notes.

Unit assessment practice

Complete a unit assessment standard:

European and World Outcome 2 requires you to draw on and apply knowledge and understanding of complex European and World historical issues in a number of ways.

Assessment standard 2.1 asks you to describe, in detail and with accuracy, the context of a European and World historical issue such as:

Describe the background to the changing attitudes towards immigrants to the USA in the 1920s.

2

Extended response practice and Top Tip 1

Top tips advise you on what markers look for in an essay and how to get good marks. A sample title is used that is a typical question in this section.

Later, at the end of other chapters you will see shorter 'top tips'. Each one goes into more detail with further examples on how to write certain sections of an extended response.

What sort of question will I be asked on this topic?

The answer to that question is easier than you might think. Setters – people who write your exam questions – **must** base their questions exactly on what is written in the SQA descriptor of what this course is about.

You already know there can only be four types of essay asked:
- To what extent … ?
- How important … ?
- A statement followed by 'How valid is that view?'
- How successfully … ?

In topic 1 you are asked to evaluate – or judge – why attitudes changed towards immigration in the 1920s. In other words, you will be asked to judge which of several reasons were the most important. There is no correct answer, so a marker is looking for you to explain all the reasons and then prioritise by deciding if the reason given to you in the question is more or less important than the others. You can make your own mind up which reason or reasons were most important. The important thing to do is make sure you have explained all possible reasons for changing attitudes towards immigration before you make your final decision in response to the question.

In this topic it is almost impossible to imagine a question that starts with 'How successfully … ?' These sorts of question are only used when the focus of the unit is on judging the effectiveness of something.

How to get good marks for your extended response

Extended responses on the subject of this book appear in Section 3 of your exam paper. Here is an example of the type of question that you could be expected to answer:

How important were economic fears in causing changing attitudes to immigration in the 1920s?

How well you will do depends on the way you respond to the question. Marks are allocated to the various sections of the response.

There are 4 marks for the **structure** of the essay. Structure refers to the introduction and conclusion of the essay. That means how you begin your essay and how you end your essay. Two marks are for the introduction and 2 marks are for the conclusion.

Structure: The Introduction

You will get up to 2 marks for your introduction if you do three things:

1 Your introduction must include a **context**. That means you must set the scene by describing the big picture or background to the issue in the question. In a couple of sentences describe the historical topic that the question is based on.

2 You need to give a **line of argument**. The simplest way to do this is to use the words in the question and include the word 'partly'. This instantly shows a marker that you are focusing on the **issue** that is being asked about but also that you are going to debate the question and examine several factors before you make your decision. In other words, you are setting out your line of argument by stating that economic fears was **one** reason but there were other reasons to consider.

So for the question above you could write: Economic fears were partly important in causing changing attitudes towards immigrants ...

3 You need to make sure that you identify other areas or factors that you are going to develop in the main part of the essay. This could be done simply as a list. So, to take our example: 'There were other factors that led to changing attitudes towards immigrants in the USA in the 1920s, such as isolationism, fear of revolution, prejudice and racism and the effects of the First World War.' This list is taken straight from the 'illustrative areas' of the syllabus on the USA available on the SQA website under Higher History (www.sqa.org.uk).

To make your introduction even better you should write a little bit more on each factor rather than just list them. To take our example again, 'However, other factors such as prejudice and racism also helped change attitudes as the type of immigrant arriving in the USA changed from the traditional 'WASP' background to a new type of immigrant from central and eastern Europe.' Expand each of the factors you have previously listed with one sentence on each and you now have a good introduction.

Now try to write the full introduction yourself.

Knowledge

Six marks are available for **relevant, detailed knowledge** that is used correctly. You will not get a mark for simply mentioning a fact. The information included has to be relevant to the question, not just the topic. One way to think about this is to use evidence to support a factor or area you are developing in the main part of your essay.

One factor you must look at in this essay is the economic fear held by Americans faced with waves of new immigrants arriving in the USA. So, here is a fact: 'New immigrants arriving in the USA were prepared to work for lower wages than Americans already in work.'

Immigration and the USA – changing attitudes

This is a fact, but it is not being used to answer the question so it needs detail and focus. Here is the fact developed and linked to the factor. 'New immigrants arriving in the USA were prepared to work for lower wages than Americans already in work, which caused attitudes towards immigrants to change and become less tolerant as American workers feared the new immigrants would take their jobs.' The fact is linked to the question, gives a little more explanation and is worth one mark. You need to do this sort of thing at least six times throughout your essay to get full marks for this.

Argument: Analysis and evaluation

Ten marks are available for the way in which you analyse and evaluate the knowledge in terms of the issue in the question asked. This means that HALF of the marks available for an extended response are for the quality of argument.

There are three different things to do to build up your marks:

1   Analyse your information by commenting on it in a basic way, but relating it more to the topic rather than the exact question – this will gain you up to 4 marks if it is done several times.

2   Develop your analysis by linking your comments about your information directly to the factor you are writing about and how it links to the question. This will allow you to be awarded up to 6 marks rather than only 4 for basic analysis.

3   Evaluate by making a judgement about the main question based on the importance of the factors or show different opinions or interpretations linked to the main question. 1–2 marks can be awarded for isolated evaluative comments AND 3–4 marks can be awarded where the candidate connects the evaluative comments together and links them to the line of argument outlined in the introduction.

Basic analysis (maximum 4 marks)

You will get up to **4 marks** if you comment on the information you have included that is relevant to the question.

So, after describing a factor, you could add a comment that links this directly to the question by adding: 'This was very effective/important because … ' By using *'because'* you are making sure that you are giving a reason, and by using judgement words like *'very effective/important'* you are giving a relative judgement about it as well.

To continue using the example above: 'Many Americans feared new immigrants would bring new political ideas from Russia into America, which led to changing attitudes towards immigrants because Americans feared the new ideas would spark off a revolution in America.'

Some comment has been made that recognises the question, but it has not addressed the focus of the issue: the 'to what extent' bit of the question. However, a basic analysis has been made.

Make this sort of comment at least four times in your essay to gain up to 4 marks.

Developed analysis can gain up to 6 marks

If your analysis comments are linked to the factor you are explaining in terms of the main question then your analysis can gain up to 6 marks, since it is more than just basic comment on importance to the topic. For example:

Many Americans feared new immigrants would bring new political ideas from Russia into America, which led to changing attitudes towards immigrants because Americans feared the new ideas would spark off a revolution in America. To a large extent the Red Scare was an important reason for changing attitudes as Americans feared new immigrants were a threat to the American political and economic system and therefore a threat to the 'American way of life'.

Notice the reference directly to the 'its importance' part of the question by the addition of the judgement. Also notice how more factual knowledge is added to support the judgement. Facts and argument go hand-in-hand.

This is a developed analysis as it relates directly to the question and provides some stronger judgement. You will get one mark for each developed analysis and if you do it at least twice in your answer you will get 2 extra marks for analysis, making a possible total of 6 marks for analysis.

Evaluation

You will get up to 4 marks for evaluating your information in terms of the question. Evaluation is the judgement you make about the relative importance of the various **factors** in terms of the question, rather than just commenting on the factual details you include about each individual factor.

To take our example once again, you could make an overall judgement that prejudice and racism was in fact the most important factor in causing changing attitudes to immigrants and that the other factors could be seen as developments or symptoms of this bigger factor. In other words, you are prioritising your factors by explaining one was more important than others.

Or you might also evaluate a factor in more depth, pointing out an alternative interpretation. For example, 'Although economic fears were important in causing changing attitudes towards immigrants, prejudice and racism were of more importance in causing Americans to be suspicious of new immigrants arriving with very different beliefs and political ideas from their own.'

Yet another way to gain evaluation marks is to compare the opinions of other historians and make a decision, with reasons, why you think one opinion is more important than another.

If you do this sort of evaluation at least four times in your essay you will get up to 4 marks.

Structure: The conclusion

The conclusion is worth up to 2 marks.

You will get 1 mark if you just summarise the information you have included in your answer.

You will get 2 marks if you can make judgements that answer the question as well as including a summary.

Here is a suggested structure that should get you 2 marks:

- 'In conclusion, there were many factors that are relevant to the question.
- On one hand … (summarise your information that links to one side of the question).
- On the other hand … (summarise opposite or different information).
- Overall, the most important … (make a judgement that directly answers the question set. By making the point that one factor is the most important you are making what is called a **relative judgement**).

Now have a go yourself. Here is a different question on this topic:

'The effects of the First World War were the main reasons for changing attitudes towards immigration in the 1920s.' How valid is this view?

Think about what you would change from the plan outlined above.

Now try to write the essay. This may not be your best essay, but lots of extended-response practice is necessary so that you produce the correct style with the correct structure under pressure in the exam.

If you find it easier at this early stage of the course to just write the introduction that is fine. In fact, writing a quick introduction to a question is a very effective way of revising and preparing for the exam. It helps you to check that you understand a topic. It is also very useful in improving your structure skills since different titles for extended responses require slightly different introductions.

Other possible questions on section 1 of the USA topic are:

1 To what extent was isolationism a main reason for changing attitudes towards immigration in the 1920s?

2 'Attitudes towards immigration were changed mostly by the effects of the First World War.' How valid is this view?

3 How important were economic fears in changing attitudes towards immigrants in 1920s USA?

Try answering these questions yourself.

At the end of the following chapters you will find other 'top tip' sections giving more detailed practical advice on the writing of introductions, the use of knowledge and basic analysis, more developed analysis and evaluation and the writing of conclusions. All of these 'top tips' will be related to content relevant to the overall topic 'The USA, 1918–1968'.

3 The struggle for civil rights

In this chapter we focus on why it was so difficult for African-Americans to gain civil rights between the years 1918 to 1941.

In 1918, most black Americans lived in the Southern states of the USA. They often lived in poverty thanks to the sharecropping system. They were discriminated against by the 'Jim Crow' laws and were terrorised by the Ku Klux Klan.

Between 1918 and 1941, when the USA joined the Second World War, thousands of black Americans migrated to the Northern cities to find a better life, yet they still suffered discrimination and persecution. It was not until the 1960s that the civil rights campaigns were successful in getting laws passed to end racial segregation and discrimination.

The background to the lack of civil rights between 1918 and 1941

For over 300 hundred years black people were abducted from Africa and taken to America where they were sold to be used as slaves for the rest of their lives. As time passed, whole generations of slaves grew up. By the 1800s most black slaves in the USA were born in America. By the 1860s there were millions of black slaves in the USA, mostly living in the South and mostly working on plantations growing cotton and tobacco.

In 1861 the American Civil War started. One reason for the war was slavery. The Northern states of the USA wanted to abolish slavery; the Southern states wanted to keep slavery. The North won the war and slavery was abolished. However, a law can stop something happening, although it cannot change attitudes and habits overnight. In the decades following the end of the Civil War in 1865, white Southerners found ways of controlling the African-American population, partly through laws and also by the use of fear and terror.

Today in the US, race is still an issue, despite improvements in the treatment of African-Americans following the civil rights campaigns of the 1960s. Movies such as *12 Years a Slave* shock many Americans who claim they have no knowledge of how African-American slaves were treated in the USA. Meanwhile, in recent years, news reports of black teenagers being beaten or shot dead by white policemen have sparked riots and protests across the country, giving rise to a new movement called Black Lives Matter. They campaign against the continuing violence and injustice faced by black people in

twenty-first-century America and elsewhere. It seems that US society is still dealing with the legacy of slavery, discrimination and segregation.

After the American Civil War most states in the South passed laws that reinforced white supremacy and discriminated against African-Americans. All these laws were called 'Jim Crow' laws. 'Jim Crow' was a nickname for all sorts of laws that treated black Americans unfairly. These 'Jim Crow' laws affected every aspect of life. Black children were forbidden to attend school with white children. Black Americans had only restricted access to public places such as parks and restaurants. At work they had separate bathrooms and collected their pay separately from whites. There were strict bans on whites and blacks marrying and cemeteries even had to provide separate graveyards.

Jim Crow laws were used to maintain a segregated society in which white authority kept control over the black population. A segregated society means one in which people of a different skin colour are kept apart.

The situation was made even worse by a decision of the Supreme Court in 1896. Homer Plessy, a fair-skinned man who only had one black ancestor (going back to his great grandparents) was refused the right to ride in a first-class rail carriage because he was black! Plessy was convicted in a Louisiana court for riding in a whites only railway car. Plessy took his case to the Supreme Court, claiming that his rights under the US Constitution were being denied.

The Supreme Court is the most important legal court in America. Its purpose is to make sure that all laws passed do not take away the basic rights of people that are guaranteed in the American constitution.

The Supreme Court judges rejected Plessy's complaint and the decision they made had long reaching consequences for African-Americans. The judges decided that segregation of black from white people was acceptable but was not meant to show that one race was better than another! The decision of the Supreme Court came to be known as the 'separate but equal' decision. The ruling legitimised Jim Crow laws throughout the USA and in effect, legalised segregation on a national scale.

Four years later, the *Richmond Times* expressed the attitude of the segregationists and the effect of the 1896 decision when it declared:

> *It is necessary that this principle be applied in every relation of Southern life. God Almighty drew the color line and it cannot be obliterated. The negro must stay on his side of the line and the white man must stay on his side, and the sooner both races recognise this fact and accept it the better it will be for both.*
>
> Richmond Times, *1900*

Mainly as a result of this ruling, segregation did not start to break down until 1954.

Source 3.1

Describe how this cartoon cleverly illustrates a criticism of the 1896 decision of separate and equal.

PLESSY VS. FERGUSON

Whites   Blacks

SEPARATE
BUT NOT EQUAL

Voting

Could African-Americans vote?

The answer is yes and no. In 1870 the Fifteenth Amendment to the US Constitution stated that the right to vote could not be denied to anyone based on their race or colour. It was therefore clear that African-American men could vote according to the Constitution. In reality, especially in the South, individual states changed their own constitutions in relation to black voters and Jim Crow laws created further obstacles to voting. Although black men had been given the right to vote in 1870, by 1900 almost no black person in the South was able to vote easily. To be able to vote in America it is necessary to register to vote but many Southern states created new voting rules which made it very difficult for black Americans to register. Examples of these voting qualifications included literacy tests, the ability to understand and explain complicated rules about the government and the introduction of a tax that had to be paid before registering to vote.

Of course, any new law in the Southern states that restricted voting on the basis of property owning or literacy would take away the rights of poor, illiterate white voters and that was unacceptable. Therefore, another rule – called the grandfather clause – allowed voting rights to those whose ancestors (for example, grandfathers) had the right to vote before the Civil War.

Naturally, since almost no African-Americans in the South had had the right to vote before the Civil War, the grandfather clause excluded them.

Although there were areas, especially in the North, where black voters elected black representatives and senators, the reality was that most African-Americans did not vote. By 1900, most African-American people still found it extremely difficult to exercise their right to vote. Partly as a result of the low numbers of black voters, politicians in the South needed to rely on the white voters. Since many of the white voters were also racist it made no political sense to campaign to help black people in the South – or even to try to stop lynching. Even Woodrow Wilson who was President in 1918 described black Americans as 'an ignorant and inferior race'.

Sharecropping

When slavery ended at the end of the Civil War, both plantation owners and ex-slaves faced problems. For the white plantation owners, they had land but could not afford to pay the ex-slaves to work on the land. For the ex-slaves, they could not afford to buy land but needed a job to survive. The solution seemed to lie in sharecropping.

Sharecropping was a system of agriculture in which a landowner allowed a tenant to use the land in return for a share of the crops produced on the land. It was also a system of farming that became very common in the South after the end of slavery and created a big obstacle to the achievement of civil rights.

Sharecropping had benefits and costs for both the owners and the sharecroppers. The landowner provided land, housing, tools and seed, and perhaps a mule – but at a cost. The sharecropper paid nothing up front, but when the harvest was collected the landowner got a *share* of the crop (about a half) and the rest of the crop was used to pay off debts to the landowner. However, the sharecropper had to pay back all his debts including the cost of equipment supplied throughout the year. The result was that the sharecropper had little left of his share of the crop so had little opportunity to save money to leave the area and find work elsewhere.

By the 1930s most African-Americans who remained in the South worked on farms and the majority of those farmers were sharecroppers. In Mississippi, 85 per cent of black farmers were sharecroppers and the peak number of sharecroppers in Tennessee was only reached in the 1930s. Sharecropping effectively kept many African-Americans in poverty or debt and hindered the campaign for civil rights since most people's energy was spent in earning enough to survive. In the 70 years since the end of the Civil War, by the mid-1930s, most African-Americans in the South had traded slavery for sharecropping, confining them still to a position of poverty and social inferiority.

The attitudes and activities of the Ku Klux Klan

The Ku Klux Klan was, and still is, a secret terrorist organisation. Started in the Southern states following the American Civil War, it had died down by the late nineteenth century. However, in 1915 the Klan was reborn, helped hugely by a newly released blockbuster movie called *The Birth of a Nation*.

Klan members had to be native-born Americans, white and Protestant. There were even special Klan sections for women. The Klan attacked any group they called 'un-American', but at heart it directed its hatred and violence primarily against African-Americans.

African-Americans in the Southern states lived in fear of lynching. Lynching meant black people being murdered by a mob who believed the black person had done something wrong. Victims were hanged and mutilated and their bodies sometimes burnt. By 1918, the Klan was known to have carried out at least 64 lynchings and 83 in 1919. Lynchings became an important obstacle in the campaign for civil rights because of the fear they instilled. Leaders of a campaign for civil rights were reluctant to step forward, and witnesses were scared to give evidence against the Klan.

Source 3.2

Poster for the film *The Birth of a Nation*.

Why do you think this movie was such an important factor in creating a major obstacle for progress towards African-American civil rights?

The federal government did almost nothing to stop lynching. The influence of the KKK also grew in Northern cities such as Detroit and Chicago as thousands of African Americans moved northwards looking for a better life. This change was called the Great Migration and we discuss this later in the chapter.

The Klan provided a sense of belonging to white 'Americans' who felt threatened by the changes around them. As new populations poured into cities, rapidly changing neighbourhoods created social tensions between ethnic groups. Most Klansmen were lower- to middle-class white people who were trying to protect their jobs and housing from the waves of newcomers to the industrial cities: immigrants from southern and eastern Europe and African-American migrants from the South. The Klan also grew in booming Southern cities such as Dallas and Houston. From their perspective, the large African-American population had to be controlled.

Klan membership had risen to 6 million by 1924, including 500,000 women. The Ku Klux Klan was THE great social organisation for much of white Protestant America in the 1920s and as membership of the Klan grew, so did its political influence. The Klan had friends in high places. In the 1920s, the Klan was powerful enough to hold large marches through Washington. Few Klansmen were arrested and in some communities, local officials even helped the Klan. In some state elections only candidates who were 'Klan-approved' were allowed to stand for election.

Source 3.3

This photo shows part of a parade by the KKK through Washington D.C.

What does the photo imply about the power and size of the Klan, given the location of the march?

Although the Klan attracted people to its ranks, most of them did not remain in the organisation for long. At its peak in the 1920s, the Klan included about 15 per cent of the nation's eligible population. However, lessening of social tensions contributed to the Klan's decline in the later 1920s. By the end of the decade, scandals involving sex and corruption had discredited the Klan, so much so that by 1929 membership had fallen to 30,000.

As immigration started to fall and fears of red revolution faded America became less tense and, it seemed, more prosperous. Nevertheless, the Ku Klux Klan remained a symbol of white terror and an important obstacle to African-Americans' civil rights.

Source 3.4

This is a photo from a race riot lynching in Omaha in 1919. How can you explain the casual and even happy expressions of some of the faces of the spectators? Should such a horrific image be used in history textbooks?

Great Migration

From 1918 onwards, many black Americans began a 'Great Migration' north looking for better wages, better jobs and an escape from segregation and fear in the South. In 1900, about 90 per cent of black Americans still lived in Southern states. Beginning in 1910, thousands of African-Americans started moving from the South to cities such as Chicago, hoping to leave behind lynchings and segregation. Cities including Detroit, Chicago and New York City had some of the biggest increases in the early part of the twentieth century. In 1910, the African-American population of Detroit was 6000. By the start of the Great Depression in 1929, the city's African-American population had increased to 120,000. Between 1910 and 1930 the African-American population in Northern states had increased by about 40 per cent.

The First World War was really the trigger for the gradual flow of African-Americans northwards to become a flood. Between 1916 and 1918 almost half a million African-Americans left the South to take advantage of labour shortages in the factories of the North. The war had almost stopped the stream of immigrants from Europe to America as it became too difficult for Eastern Europeans to cross the war zones of Europe. After the war, when new laws reduced immigration to a trickle, even more African-Americans seized the opportunity to move North in search of well-paid factory jobs.

The Great Migration was the chance that black Americans had been awaiting since the end of the Civil War. Life was better in the North, there was no Klan and no Jim Crow laws – or so they thought. However, for many African-Americans problems did not vanish – they simply became different problems.

Source 3.5

The Great Migration from the South to the North and West of USA.

In the nineteenth century the industrial cities of the North had been the destination for thousands of European immigrants. Now, with the Great Migration, thousands of African-Americans from the South settled next to the neighbourhoods of European immigrants on Chicago's South Side, near jobs in the stockyards and meatpacking plants. Between 1916 and 1919 the African-American population in Chicago increased from 44,000 to 109,000. The rapid influx of migrants led to racial tension as competition for jobs and housing increased. White property owners and real estate agents refused to sell housing to African-Americans, who consequently found themselves segregated into communities and areas of cities known as ghettos.

Source 3.6

Book cover of *The Great Migration, Journey to the North*.

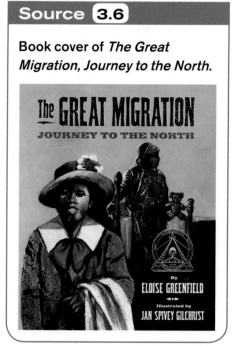

The tensions created by the Great Migration and made worse by a lack of adequate housing resulted in several race riots in Northern cities such as Washington and Chicago. As early as 1919 racial tensions in Chicago were obvious. On 27 July 1919 a race riot began which ended with 38 people dead and over 500 injured. The Chicago riot was the worst of 25 other riots that took place in Northern cities, reflecting the tension and intolerance within the USA at the end of the First World War.

Although there were no Jim Crow laws or formal segregation in the Northern cities, it is clear that informal segregation did exist and that African-Americans still faced huge difficulties.

Source 3.7

How important was the Great Migration in improving the treatment of African-Americans after 1918?

The Great Migration did help some black Americans to improve their lives. However, the bulk of African-Americans lived in the Southern states and their lives remained mostly unchanged. For example, in Mississippi the African-American population had been 56 per cent of the entire population in 1910 and still stood at 32 per cent in 1940. When the Second World War ended in 1945 the vast majority of black Americans still suffered from prejudice, discrimination and fear. The loss of so many thousands of African-Americans who were prepared to take risks to improve their lives 'up north' robbed the South of potential leaders and campaigners in the future. Put simply, those African-Americans who had the 'get up and go' to perhaps change things in the South simply got up and went to the North.

On the other hand, the numbers of African-Americans living in Northern cities did increase hugely. The creation of 'black metropolises' created a base and a market for African-American newspapers, businesses, jazz clubs, churches and political organisations that provided the launchpad for civil rights campaigns that would grow in the 1950s. It was in the cities, especially New York's Harlem, that the ideas of Black Pride and black identity first developed by Marcus Garvey took root. We will look at this in the next section.

Divided organisations, limited progress

In the years following the Supreme Court decision of 1896, African-Americans did not just accept segregation and discrimination as inevitable or normal. Several organisations were formed to campaign for improvements in the lives of African-Americans. Later, these aims to improve living and working conditions would combine into a Civil Rights Movement – but not yet.

There were three main black American leaders, each with very different ideas about how to win improvements, and these differences of opinions were perhaps also another obstacle in gaining civil rights.

Their differences can be summed up as:

1 Should African-Americans be persuaded that only hard work and education would win civil rights for some and that progress would be slow?

2 Should African-Americans claim civil rights immediately as American citizens and fight for civil rights through the law courts?

3 Should African-Americans be encouraged to reject white society and campaign for their right to be separate and even to return to their ethnic roots in Africa?

Group 1: Booker T. Washington and the Tuskegee Institute

Although Booker T. Washington is mostly forgotten about now, between 1890 and 1915, he was the most important leader in the African-American community, but his ideas caused bitter arguments. Born in 1856, and the son of a slave, Booker T. Washington became well known as a teacher and developed the Tuskegee Institute in Alabama. The Tuskegee Institute specialised in industrial and agricultural training of African-Americans. All this fitted in with Washington's main belief which was that African-Americans should first be trained for trades before fighting for civil rights and equality. In the early 1900s he argued that African-Americans could only advance if they were educated.

Source 3.8

Booker T. Washington

'Success is not to be measured so much by the position that one has reached in life but by the obstacles which he has overcome while trying to succeed.'

Washington's policy of slow improvement and his opposition to trying to change Jim Crow laws or gain civil rights, meant accepting that African-Americans would not be treated equally by the white population for years to come. In fact, Washington was accused of being an 'Uncle Tom' which was an insult at that time because it meant an African-American who was too eager to do what white people told him to do. This opinion of Booker T. Washington was reinforced: by a speech he made in 1895 that became known as the Atlanta Compromise

 You can be sure in the future, as in the past, that you and your [white] families will be surrounded by the most patient, faithful, law-abiding, and unresentful people that the world has seen.'

In effect, Washington was promising that African-Americans would accept their lower social position and would be no threat to white-controlled society and would not want to change it. As a result, Southern whites, who had previously been against the education of African-Americans, now supported Washington's ideas as they saw them as means of encouraging African-Americans to accept their inferior economic and social position in society.

The Atlanta speech angered other African-American leaders such as William Du Bois of the NAACP (see later) because Booker T. Washington stated that African-Americans would only be ready to be considered equal to white Americans **after** they had 'improved themselves' by hard work and education. Washington's message was that it was not the time to challenge Jim Crow segregation and the problems faced by black voters in the South. Instead, he argued that the surest way for African-Americans to gain equal rights was first of all to demonstrate 'industry, thrift, intelligence and property'.

Washington argued that conflict with the white population would lead to disaster and that co-operation with whites who wanted to support the African-American community was the only way to overcome racism in the long run. Washington wrote:

 Any attempt to improve the Negro South, must have as one of its aims making the Negro able to live in a friendly and peaceable way with his white neighbors. In spite of all talk of moving north, the Negro's home is permanently in the South. It is our duty to help him prepare himself to live there an independent, educated citizen.

Washington also spoke out against the appeal of Marcus Garvey and his UNIA (see later). He said:

 I see no way out of the Negro's condition in the South by returning to Africa. Aside from other huge obstacles, there is no place in Africa for him to go where his condition would be improved . Even famous explorers of Africa tell me that they know of no place in Africa where the Negroes of the United States might go to advantage.

It should now be clear that the followers of Booker T. Washington's ideas were not going to campaign for civil rights. At the same time, other African-American organisations took root and they disagreed greatly with Booker T. Washington. In the years after 1918, the different opinions in the African-American community on how best to achieve civil rights was a major obstacle to an effective campaign.

Group 2: The National Association for the Advancement of Colored People (NAACP)

By the 1890s, many Southern states had introduced Jim Crow laws and made it much more difficult for African-Americans to vote. For example, black Americans in Mississippi who had been voting for 30 years were suddenly told they did not 'qualify' for the vote. It seemed that Southern law-makers were making life harder for black Americans by removing civil rights gained after the Civil War. In 1905, a group of African-American leaders met to discuss these problems. The group of leaders became known as the Niagara Movement because they met on the Canadian side of the Niagara river. Had they met on the US side they would not have been allowed in the hotel because it would have been segregated.

The Niagara Movement called for an end to racial segregation and disenfranchisement (the taking away of the right to vote). The Movement

also aimed to advance the interest of black citizens; to secure for them the right to vote, to increase their opportunities for securing justice in the courts, to provide education for the children and to ensure complete equality before law.

In February 1909, from the ashes of the Niagara Movement, the National Association for the Advancement of Colored People (NAACP) was born, with W.E.B. Du Bois its most famous leader. Du Bois totally rejected the idea that African-Americans were in any way inferior to whites – a position that brought him into conflict with the ideas of Booker T. Washington. In 1910, Du Bois and 22 other African-Americans issued a statement directly attacking the ideas of Washington:

> *We regret to say that Mr. Booker T Washington is giving the impression that the Negro problem in America is moving towards a satisfactory solution. He is giving an impression which is not true. His program of industrial education, conciliation of the South, and submission and silence as to civil and political rights is wrong. Today in eight states where the bulk of the Negroes live, black men of property and university training can be, and usually are, by law denied the ballot, while the most ignorant white man votes.*

Source 3.9

W.E.B. Du Bois

'A little less complaint and whining and a little more dogged work and manly striving, would do us more credit than a thousand civil rights bills.'

The main aims of the NAACP were to gain the vote for all male 'Negro-Americans'. It also called for equal treatment for all American citizens alike and wanted an end to the sharecropping system, which was described by the NAACP as 'virtual slavery'. To achieve its aims the NAACP used legal action in its fight to improve employment, housing, voting and education.

In its early years, the NAACP challenged various Jim Crow laws and campaigned against President Woodrow Wilson's introduction of racial segregation into federal government in 1913. By 1914, the NAACP had grown to 6000 members and 50 branches and achieved a victory in winning the right of African-Americans to serve as officers in the First World War. This led to 600 African-American officers and 700,000 men registering for the draft. Within the ranks of the African-American forces Big Jim Europe and his Hellcat Jazzmen kept the new fashion for jazz alive with their wartime music. You can still see and hear them on YouTube.

The NAACP also led African-American protests against the biggest movie of the time, *The Birth of a Nation*. While white audiences crowded to see the film, the NAACP complained that the film was offensive to African-Americans, especially as it showed the Ku Klux Klan as a heroic organisation saving America. However, throughout the 1920s and 1930s, the main focus of the NAACP was to try to stop lynching, but it was not successful. For most African-Americans during this period, the NAACP was an organisation dominated by prosperous middle-class blacks of the North, who had little in common with poverty-stricken Southern communities. It was not until the Civil Rights Movement of the 1950s and 1960s that the NAACP was seen as a significant force in the civil rights campaign.

Group 3: Marcus Garvey and the Universal Negro Improvement Association (UNIA)

In 1914, a new and much more radical organisation was started. It was called the Universal Negro Improvement Association – UNIA for short – and was led by Marcus Garvey, whose ideas were almost the exact opposite of both Washington's and Du Bois'.

Garvey was a Jamaican-born black nationalist who moved to Harlem, New York in 1916. The following year he set up the New York division of the UNIA just as the African-American population of the city was growing as a result of the Great Migration. Within three months, membership of the UNIA had reached 3500. Huge processions of organised UNIA members in uniforms impressed the thousands of onlookers. Garvey had trained himself to be an excellent public speaker and for a short time the UNIA became the biggest and best known African-American organisation. In 1919, Garvey started his own newspaper, *Negro World*, in which he encouraged African-Americans to be proud of their race and their culture.

Garvey also advocated returning to roots in Africa, their ancestral homeland, long before the Black Power movement of the 1960s and echoed in Bob Marley's anthemic song 'Exodus' from 1977. (See: **https://www.youtube.com/watch?v=43cfPgZ8cU8**)

To help in his dream of a return to Africa, Garvey even started the Black Star Line in 1919 to provide steamship transportation to Africa. He claimed it was a luxury shipping company but in reality it had one ship, a converted coal carrier. And that summed up Garvey. His flamboyant dress style, with flashy uniforms and feathered hats, was an early version of what Michael Jackson wore in the 1980s; Garvey was a showman. He attracted huge publicity (in 1920 Garvey claimed a UNIA membership of 2 million), but he also caused fear among the white authorities and that was his undoing.

Historians now believe that the popularity of Garvey's call for blacks to establish a home in Africa and of his attempts to adopt the ceremonial style and dress of whites was a sign of frustration with the slow pace of the NAACP campaign. However, at the time, the federal government were alarmed by a city-based, organised, militant and large African-American organisation. The FBI investigated him and planted the first African-American FBI agent in the leadership of the UNIA. Some claim Garvey was set up but whatever the truth, Garvey was arrested on fraud charges in 1922 and deported from the USA in 1925.

Source 3.10

Marcus Garvey

'A people without knowledge of their past history, origins and culture is like a tree without roots.'

Now that you have found out something about the main three civil rights organisations and their leaders, which of the three would you have supported and why? Why would you have rejected the other two?

These divisions between the African-American organisations caused their own difficulties. Differences between the aims and methods of organisations divided support. In a way, these problems became obstacles in the path of civil rights because the different organisations prevented the growth of a single organised protest movement.

On balance, although Booker T. Washington's ideas seemed the most passive and unlikely to change anything quickly, it is also true to say that Washington was the most realistic. The UNIA and NAACP did little to help the real problems of poverty and unemployment facing African-Americans in the 1920s and 1930s.

For anyone growing up in the South in the 1920s and 1930s, racism, segregation and unfair discrimination were completely normal – and that was part of the problem. It would be wrong to think of white society in the South as evil. Such an idea would not enter the heads of most white Southerners – even those who attended lynchings. Life in the South had been shaken by the Civil War and the ending of slavery but attitudes, culture and expectations had not changed. African-Americans were still 'blacks' and whites were naturally the superior race. Any attempt to change that would have been very difficult.

White society was not ready to change and without federal government little change was possible. No President of the USA was prepared to sacrifice immensely important political support in the South for the sake of black civil rights, especially as support for segregation was growing in the North and West as well. Compared with the serious issues of the 1920s and 1930s – prohibition, organised crime and the Depression – the issue of civil rights did not seem worth the trouble.

The 'Scottsboro Boys'

There are many examples of racist attitudes in the South in the 1920s and 1930s – one example involved the 'Scottsboro Boys'.

On 25 March 1931 nine young African-American men between the ages of 12 and 21 rode a freight train away from their home in Chattanooga, Tennessee. Several white teenagers jumped off the train and reported to the sheriff that they had been attacked by a group of black teenagers. By the end of the day all nine of the young black men had been taken off the train by a sheriff's gang and charged with raping two white girls. This was the beginning of a long legal case that highlighted the racism, prejudice and discrimination that existed in parts of the USA in the 1930s.

The case became known as the 'Scottsboro Boys' because Scottsboro was the town in Alabama where they were on trial for the first time. The boys all said they were not guilty but their plea was immediately rejected by the

Extended response practice and Top Tip 2

Writing a successful introduction

At the end of Chapter 2 you may have seen a top tip providing general advice on how to write a good extended response. At the end of this chapter and all the others in this book you will find more top tips giving more detailed advice about certain parts of your extended response. This top tip is about writing a good introduction.

The examples provided here all relate to the SQA mandatory content topic:

> 'An evaluation of the obstacles to the achievement of civil rights for black Americans up to 1941'.

When you are preparing for the exam think very carefully about the style of question you will be asked and what the question will be about. In this case ALL the extended response questions will be about the issue mentioned above. In simple English the issue means – what were the most important things that stopped black Americans getting better treatment before 1941?

There is nothing special about the date 1941. It is just when America joined the Second World War, so this section is only about things that affected black Americans in the 1920s and 1930s.

To be sure about what questions you might be asked on the USA topic, check with the SQA website (www.sqa.org.uk/sqa/47923.html). The detail for Section 2 of the USA topic is: 'Legal impediments, the separate but equal decision of the supreme court, popular prejudice, the lack of political influence and finally divisions within the black community.' All of these things can be thought of as obstacles to the achievement of civil rights for black Americans up to 1941.

You should also know about the style of question you will be asked. There are only four styles of question you can be asked:

1 One style is to start with 'To what extent ... ' such as: 'To what extent were the activities of the Ku Klux Klan the main reason why Black Americans did not gain civil rights before 1941?'

2 Another style is to provide a statement, such as why there was so little progress in civil rights before 1941 and then follow with a second sentence that states, 'How valid is that view?' An example would be: 'The Separate but Equal decision of the Supreme Court was the most important obstacle in preventing black Americans from achieving civil rights before 1941.' How valid is that view?

3 The third style is to ask how important something was – for example 'How important were divisions within the black community in preventing black Americans from achieving civil rights before 1941?'

4 Finally, there is a fourth style of question that asks, 'How successfully did someone or something deal with a problem or difficulty?' This is an unlikely style of question for this section because the focus is on the problems and difficulties facing black Americans and no question in this section can ask how effective or successful something was in helping progress towards civil rights.

Now start planning an introduction to this question:

'The Ku Klux Klan was the most important obstacle in preventing Black Americans from achieving civil rights before 1941.' How valid is that view?

First of all think about the **topic**. What do you have to know about to answer this question? You might think the answer is obvious, and it is! But under exam pressure people can become confused and lose marks and time by writing about irrelevant subjects. So the **topic** of this question is about black Americans and the problems they faced in the 1920s and 1930s.

The next thing to think about is the **task**. In other words, what you have to do to answer the question successfully. You have been given the opinion that the Ku Klux Klan was the most important problem facing black Americans in the 1920s and 1930s. You are then asked if that opinion is 'valid' which means 'Is it correct?' How you answer this question is almost exactly the same as how you answer any other question on this topic.

Remember your introduction must have a context, a line of argument and at least a mention of the factors you will develop in your essay.

First of all, your introduction should have a **context**. Do not spend too long on it. It should take about two sentences although it can be done in one. In context your introduction should briefly outline the background to the question. In this case outline how black Americans were so badly treated in the 1920s and 1930s. You must include relevant information so a brief description of the situation black Americans lived in could be something like this:

Although slavery had been abolished long before the 1920s, black Americans still suffered persecution and discrimination thanks to the Jim Crow laws. By the 1920s and 1930s most black Americans, especially in the South, had little freedom and many lived in fear.

That's all you need for a context – two sentences.

Next you need a **line of argument**. Your argument should always open out your answer so you can write about the main factor mentioned in the title (the KKK) but also you should write about other problems, or obstacles, facing black progress to civil rights. An easy way to do this is to say that the idea given to you in the question is *partly* important but that there are other reasons which also need to be considered.

technology. In *The Grapes of Wrath* John Steinbeck wrote about the impact of change on the family farms of the Midwest:

 The land companies – that's another name for the banks that owned the land – want tractors, not families on the land. Is a tractor bad? Is the power that turns the long furrows wrong? If our tractor turned the long furrows of our land, it would be good. But the tractor does two things – it turns the land and turns us off the land.

By the mid-1920s, European agriculture had recovered and American farmers found it more difficult to find export markets for their goods. The decline in agricultural profits meant that many farmers had difficulty paying the heavy mortgages on their farms. By the 1930s many American farmers were in serious financial difficulties

2 Traditional industries

Another group of Americans who did not prosper from the boom years of the 1920s were those who worked in the older industries, especially coal mining and cotton mills. Workers in old traditional industries were already disadvantaged by their inability to form trade unions to bargain for higher wages and better conditions. The ideologies of rugged individualism combined with laissez-faire government policies meant that big business owners would smash attempts to form workplace unions. Politically and socially, the idea of trade unions also had little support from the bulk of Americans who suspected such trade unions as being a cover for anarchism and revolution. Remember the 1920s was also the time of the Red Scare, with new immigrants arriving with potentially dangerous ideas. With no strong voice or organisation to assist coal miners, overproduction and falling demand resulted in wage cuts, longer working hours and increasingly dangerous working conditions as employers cut back on spending and cut corners which endangered miners' safety.

The 1920s also brought new challenges to the older industries. Coal mining faced competition from new power sources such as oil, gas and electricity, while cotton production suffered from changes in both fashion and textile technology. Before 1918 coal output soared until 680 million tons were produced in that year, but by 1932 production had fallen to 360 million tons. In personal terms, a coal miner's wage in 1929 was barely a third of the national average income. For an even more detailed comparison, while the average monthly income of a New York bricklayer in 1929 was around $320, coal miners earned only $103 a month. The cotton industry also faced a challenge, not only from new technology but also from fashion changes. The fashion of the 'flappers' of the 1920s was for short hair and

shorter dresses with no petticoats. For men, it was a habit to wear a cotton vest under a shirt but when a movie called *It Happened One Night* revealed the no-vest hairy chest of the mega star Clark Gable, the sales of men's cotton vests collapsed immediately!

The impact of movies and fashion magazines hit cotton cloth production at the same time as new synthetic materials like nylon and rayon were replacing cotton in the wardrobes and catwalks of fashion conscious America. The new, cheaper materials allowed even poorer Americans to have a change of clothing and copies of the latest styles, as advertised in the mail order catalogues and the cinemas being built in every small town.

Like the coal industry, cotton mill workers had no bargaining power and their area of work, mainly in the South, was far from the booming cities of the North. In 1926 the average weekly wage of a New York City worker was $200 per week. In Loray Cotton Mill, North Carolina male workers earned $18 per week. Women only earned half of that amount. In the Northern states some cotton mills tried to improve pay and conditions but economic reality still had to be faced. How could those better mills compete against harsh mills in the South that still used child labour on starvation wages?

3 African-Americans, Native Americans and new immigrants

The other significant groups that did not prosper during the boom years of the 1920s were African-Americans, Native Americans and the new immigrants huddled in the ghetto tenements around New York.

The difficulties faced by African-Americans in the 1920s have been described in Chapter 3 but some more details will add to the realisation of just how far African-Americans were 'outside' the prosperity of the 1920s. During that time three-quarters of a million black farm workers lost their jobs. For those who were successful in finding a $5 a day job in the Ford car factory, life was better, but most African-American migrants only found a life in slum ghettos and the most basic low paid jobs. Even at the height of the Great Migration 85 per cent of African-American still lived in the South, many working as sharecroppers and experiencing the life of poverty that made up that existence (for more details on sharecropping as it affected African-Americans see Chapter 3).

Native Americans are still most commonly, if wrongly, called Red Indians. During the nineteenth century, white America spread west, justified by its belief in manifest destiny. This was a belief that the Christian God had given settlers the right to settle and develop all the land and resources of the USA. As a result, the Native American Nations (called tribes) were forcibly moved onto reservations. These reservations were often on the poorest quality land many hundreds of miles from the homelands of the dispossessed. A series of wars against the Native American tribes in the later nineteenth century was almost a policy of race genocide and when that failed to wipe out the Native

Americans completely, then followed a systematic policy of erasing Native American culture. Finally, it was not until 1924 that a law even recognised Native Americans as full citizens of the USA. However, by that time reservation life had reduced the population of 'Red Indians' to an easily forgotten minority suffering long-term unemployment and alcoholism. Those people did not benefit from the boom.

Why was there a crash in 1929?

The usual story of the USA in the 1920s describes how the Wall Street Crash of October 1929 suddenly brought an end to the 'roaring 20s' as if the crisis of 1929 came from nowhere and caught everyone by surprise. However, recent historians have questioned that simple story. They argue that the foundations of US prosperity were weak and that beneath the advertising gloss of 'boom times' the harsh reality of overproduction, a saturated market and underconsumption were all storing up trouble for the future. Critics of the US economy in the 1920s also point to a lack of understanding of how economics works. Economists and historians such as J.K. Galbraith and Arthur Schlesinger blame the government for a deadly combination of laissez-faire when more control would have been helpful and a policy of protectionism that led almost immediately to problems for the USA when other countries retaliated with their own tariff barriers. In *The Penguin History of the United States of America*, Hugh Brogan blamed the Republican policies for 'a bland unawareness of economic and political essentials'. Those historians and economists argue that the government, banks and big business should have seen the crash coming since the boom years of the 1920s rested on very weak foundations, not just the artificial prosperity of the consumer boom.

The first of those weak foundations was the banking system. In the 1920s there was no control over banks. Anyone could open a bank and in hundreds of small communities local people put their money into the banks for safekeeping and a small amount of interest. The banks then used that money to make investments that made some money for the banks.

The problem was that as the economic boom grew, banks began to invest savers' money in stocks and shares, hoping to make a large profit for themselves by selling the same stocks and shares when prices rose. After all, that was what had been happening year after year in the late 1920s. But what would happen if share prices started to fall? What would happen if savers suddenly wanted their savings back from banks that had been gambling on share prices rising?

When the crash did happen, savers did want their money back. Banks could not cope with the demand. They closed. Panic spread as savers wanted their own money back in their possession. The normal banking system almost ceased to exist, and without a stable and efficient banking system the economy could not function properly.

International problems

The government's policy of protective tariffs was meant to help the US economy by making foreign imports more expensive. Americans would therefore choose to buy the relatively cheaper American-made products. The aim was to cope with the problems of overproduction and underconsumption. In the short term these tariffs helped American companies prosper. But in the longer term foreign countries fought back by placing high tariff taxes on American goods, thus making it harder for American companies to sell what they made. In effect, countries around the world stopped buying American goods.

In reality, protectionism made the US economy worse. Foreign countries were angered by America's tariff barriers so they raised taxes on American goods arriving in their country. The Republicans had no answer to falling demand, and the continuing reliance on higher tariffs to protect American products, such as the Hawley Smoot Act of 1930, ignored the reality of the situation. Despite protectionism making American goods comparatively cheaper, people had little money to spend and American exports were hit when other countries raised their own tariff barriers in retaliation.

The Wall Street Crash

During the 1920s, there was a rapid rise in the value of stocks and shares on the New York Stock Exchange, based in Wall Street in New York. Businesses raise money by selling shares. A share in a business means the buyer gets a share in the profits of the business. As the business makes money and becomes more valuable so the price of a share goes up. In the late 1920s it seemed as if every business in America was making money and everybody wanted a share of the profits. Buyers chased shares and as a result share prices went up. Rising share prices made it look as if a business really was doing well. High share prices across Wall Street made it look as if the whole US economy was doing well. However, the whole system was based on confidence – confidence that the boom would continue and that share prices would keep going up.

Confidence in the economic boom in the USA had increased after Hoover's election victory in 1928, encouraged by optimistic speeches about the ending of poverty and the promise of everlasting prosperity. Buying shares seemed like an easy way to make money. Buy the shares, wait a few days, and then sell at a profit as share prices increase. Many people became overconfident and borrowed money to buy shares. The trick was to sell shares just before the price started to fall.

The Wall Street Crash had been predicted, but the warnings were ignored in a collective rush to 'get rich quick', with people buying and selling shares

for big profits. Everyone wanted a piece of the action. Under normal circumstances in a stable economy, stocks and shares were bought and sold by a few businessmen in Wall Street and a few offices scattered across the USA. In 1919 there were 500 such stockbroking firms across the USA. By 1928 that number had increased to 1192. In June 1929 the 'value' of shares on the stock market reached new heights – but what was value? The value of shares are meant to represent the real value of the company, but the demand for shares from speculators kept pushing up share prices, making companies seem more valuable than they really were.

There was no official control over the Wall Street Stock Exchange. Anyone could buy shares and by 1929 tens of thousands of people were buying 'on the margin' which meant large numbers of shares could be bought with a small cash deposit and the balance made up by borrowing money. Naturally the borrowed money would be paid back when the shares were sold at a high profit – at least that was the plan.

Then something strange happened. Some investors grew suspicious that share prices could not rise forever and became nervous – and started to sell their shares.

On Saturday 19 October 1929, four million shares were bought and sold. The next day – a Sunday – when the market was closed, newspapers reported falling share prices. Investors knew that if the selling continued the next day then the value of their shares could fall dramatically. For many investors it was vital to sell their shares as fast as they could on the Monday morning. Within four days over 20 million shares were sold and on Black Thursday – 24 October 1929 – share prices fell so fast that panic spread. The following day representatives of the top banks made a big show of buying shares in an attempt to calm things down and even the President tried to convince people that 'the business of the country is on a sound and prosperous basis'. But all attempts to stabilise the stock market failed and on Tuesday 29 October the market crashed. Almost 17 million shares were traded in one day. Often no buyers for shares could be found at all. Total panic set in. Thousands of people faced losing ALL their money as share prices collapsed. Even worse, for the tens of thousands who had bought shares 'on the margin', they now had to repay the loans they had taken out to pay for shares that were now totally worthless.

Was the Wall Street Crash the cause of the Great Depression?

Historians now mostly agree that the Wall Street Crash was not the cause of the Depression. What the Wall Street Crash *did* do was reveal just how fragile and unstable the boom of the 1920s really was. Businessmen who had been investing for years saw danger signs with the problems of a saturated market, overproduction and underconsumption. They could see the nonsense of America giving loans to Europe so Europe could use the same money to repay debts to America. The businessmen could see that

small investors, greedy to 'get rich quick', were artificially pushing share prices up by the simple law of supply and demand – as demand increases so does price. It has nothing to do with the real value of the economy.

Source 4.6

Find and select your own set of images that best capture the shock and consequences of the Wall Street Crash.

You can decide what format you want – perhaps hard-copy poster or PowerPoint. Be prepared to justify your selection.

What the crash did mean was that tens of thousands of small private individuals had gambled – and lost. Under the confident consumer boom of the 1920s the danger signs had been ignored. The speculators of 1929 had forgotten or ignored the golden rule of investments: that prices can go up as well as down. Banks which had invested customers' money in shares lost a fortune. In a desperate attempt to survive, the banks called in any outstanding loans to customers. As news spread of the banks' difficulties, people rushed to take their savings out of the banks. In 1929 over 650 banks went bust and that number rose to 2294 banks in 1931.

With loans called in by banks many companies also went bankrupt. Between 1929 and 1932 almost 110,000 separate businesses failed. Factories closed as the consumer boom collapsed. This led to increasing unemployment. In 1929 just over 3 per cent of the workforce in the USA were unemployed. By 1933 that figure had risen to 25 per cent. That caused serious poverty for millions of Americans. In February 1933 *New Republic* magazine reported:

> *Last summer in the hot weather, when the smell was sickening and the flies were thick there were hundreds of people coming to the dumps every day. A widow fed herself and her 14-year-old son on garbage. Before she picked up food thrown away she always took off her glasses so she could not see the maggots.*

New Republic *magazine 1933*

Tens of thousands of people who had enjoyed the consumer boom were now homeless and destitute. Those who could not pay rent were evicted, while homeowners could not afford mortgages and had to sell their homes. Many people lived in shacks made from packing cases and corrugated iron and others slept on park benches. Many blamed President Hoover, who had promised everlasting prosperity. The new President unwittingly gave rise to a new vocabulary: newspapers used to cover people sleeping rough were called Hoover blankets and the shacks of the destitute were called Hoovervilles.

The real importance of the Wall Street Crash lay in the shock to confidence. Experts did not believe that lasting financial damage had been done. Even after October 1929, prices still stood higher than they had during the previous year. What had been wiped out was the spectacular rise in share price over the previous nine months.

Source 4.7

There are many images like this. Would it be too simplistic to say that such images show the consequences of the Wall Street Crash?

How might you disagree with the simplicity of such a statement?

The crash and the Depression were the result of long-term problems and Republican policies were not entirely to blame. However, while President Hoover's representative said that prosperity was 'just around the corner', the Republicans did little to help the economy recover.

Between 1929 and 1932, over 100,000 businesses collapsed and 15 million people became unemployed, losing not only their jobs, but their savings and their homes as well. For a while politicians believed that the economy would eventually recover by itself without the need for federal intervention, but even President Hoover forced the federal government to do far more than would have been thought possible in the early 1920s in order to fight the economic crisis. However, federal spending on job creation was far outweighed by cutbacks at state and local level. Overall, Republican attempts to take America out of the Depression were described as 'too little too late'.

In the American political system, elections for President are held every four years. Herbert Hoover had been elected in 1928. He had announced that America was near to removing poverty from the nation and had promised the prosperity of the boom years would continue. However, as the date of the next election approached in 1932, the USA was in the grip of a depression. Confidence in the future was shattered and millions of Americans began to look for someone other than Herbert Hoover and the Republicans to get them out of the mess they were in.

Think about and create 4.8

'In America today we are nearer to a final triumph over poverty than in any other land.'

What evidence would supporters of Hoover use to support the statement?

What evidence would opponents of Hoover use to attack the statement?

Nevertheless, it is important to establish that FDR and his New Deal **did** change the USA, it **did** help the people of the USA in the short term and it **did** help the USA recover in the longer term.

The phrase New Deal is taken from a speech made by FDR when he promised 'a new deal for the American people'. That is very different from having a carefully worked out plan of action. FDR did promise 'action, and action now', but he did not make clear what that action would be. In reality, the New Deal was a rush of new laws and new government agencies set up to deal with the problems of the Depression as and when needed – and most of these ideas were needed fast!

The presidential campaign of 1932 had been chiefly a debate over the causes and possible solutions to the problems of the Great Depression. On the one hand, the incumbent President Hoover tried to remain optimistic but held firm to his belief that the solution to the Depression lay in rugged individualism and hard work. On the other hand, his Democratic opponent, Franklin Delano Roosevelt, believed that the government should take action and give direct help to individuals to see them through the worst times and to give them hope for the future.

In the US political system there is a gap – referred to as the presidential transition – between the time of the Presidential election result and the point at which the victor takes office. In the election of 8 November 1932, Hoover lost to Roosevelt. However, Roosevelt did not take over as President until 4 March 1933, at the very height of the Depression.

The New Deal

Source 5.2

A cartoon of FDR carrying a bin of policies while Herbert Hoover (HH) walks away.
Explain as fully as you can how this cartoon illustrates the difference in policies and attitudes between the Republicans, led by Hoover, and the Democrats, led by Roosevelt. Try to comment on at least six features in the cartoon.

He told Americans that the only thing they had to fear was fear itself and offered a 'new deal for the American people'.

Before becoming President, Roosevelt had been governor of New York State and had used his position directly to help the thousands of people thrown into poverty by the Depression. He believed he knew what the people needed and also what was needed for the USA. Essentially, this was to restore **confidence**. FDR lost no time and in his inaugural speech he provided the first of many famous sound bites:

> " *Let me assert my firm belief that the only thing we have to fear is … fear itself — nameless, unreasoning, unjustified terror which paralyzes needed efforts to convert retreat into advance … This Nation asks for action, and action now … Our greatest primary task is to put people to work … We must act and act quickly.*

Source 5.3

FDR's first 100 days – Action, and action now.

Explain the visual content and words of this poster and cartoon within the context of the Depression and Roosevelt's victory in the Presidential election.

Roosevelt's inaugural speech was an inspirational turning point in American history. In just a few minutes Roosevelt achieved what Hoover had failed to do in the previous four years: he gave people confidence that something could be done to move America out of the Depression. In the election campaign, Roosevelt had offered hope rather than specific remedies to the 12 million unemployed, and in the election FDR won 57 per cent of the popular vote and was victor in all but six of the 50 states.

Unit assessment practice

Complete a unit assessment standard:

> European and World Outcome 1 requires you to evaluate the factors contributing to historical developments in a number of ways.

> Assessment standard 1.3 asks you to use detailed evidence to support a conclusion.

An example might be:

Come to a conclusion on what you consider to be the most important reasons why America recovered from its economic problems in the 1930s and explain why you reached this conclusion.

Extended response practice and Top Tip 4

This top tip provides advice on how to gain marks for basic analysis and analysis plus marks. Within the total marks available for your extended response (essay) you can gain 4 marks for basic analysis and an extra 2 marks for analysis plus. Please **do not** worry about evaluation marks in this section. Evaluation marks are part of top tip 5.

All the examples here apply to the SQA mandatory content topic:

> 'An assessment of the effectiveness of the New Deal'.

In this section you are asked to assess – or judge – how effective the New Deal was. In order to judge the success – or effectiveness – of the New Deal you must look at what the New Deal was meant to do. Check that for yourself in this chapter. The most obvious answer is that the New Deal was meant to help the American people and the US economy recover from the economic depression of the early 1930s. There is no one correct answer so a marker is looking for you to know what the New Deal did and be able to judge how successful the New Deal was.

When you are preparing for the exam think very carefully about the style of question you will be asked and what the question will be about. In this case **all** the extended response questions will be about the issue mentioned above. In simple English the issue means – what was the New Deal and how good was it at helping the US recover from the economic crises of the early 1930s?

What sort of question will I be asked?

Unlike previous sections, extended response questions on this topic can easily start with 'How successful' because the focus of the unit is on judging the effectiveness of the New Deal.

You should already know the other types of extended response questions that can be asked in this section so remind yourself how the following words

form part of the three types of questions apart from 'How successfully'. The words are **extent**, **valid** and **important**. Make up three questions relevant to this section and with each question using one of the words from the list.

Possible questions on topic 4 are:

1 To what extent was the role of Roosevelt in confidence building the main reason for the effectiveness of the New Deal?

2 'The New Deal was not the total success many people claimed it to be.' How valid is that view?

3 How important was the role of federal government to the effectiveness of the New Deal?

4 How successfully did the first New Deal achieve its aims of relief, recovery and reform?

Remember! If there is a question on this New Deal section you will only get **one** question on the topic. In fact there might be **no** question on this topic since there will only be three questions on the USA topic taken from the six possible sections.

How do I get good marks for basic analysis?

There are four marks available for basic analysis and an extra two marks for developed analysis. To get the marks available you should aim to do two things. The first is to make a straightforward comment on the importance of your information in terms of what the question is about. For example, if you include some factual information about the New Deal such as 'President Roosevelt began a series of fireside chats to explain to the American people what the New Deal was going to do,' then you will gain a knowledge mark. However, you can easily get a basic analysis mark by adding the word 'because' then giving a reason why the fireside chats became an important part of the New Deal.

You could write something like this: 'President Roosevelt began a series of fireside chats in which FDR explained to the American people what the New Deal was going to do. This was important to the New Deal because it gave people confidence that the President was doing something positive to help them.' This shows how a basic analysis comment can be linked to information you have included.

The comment is basic analysis because it is relevant to the subject of the question but it does not focus on the issue, which means it does not try to answer the 'To what extent … ' or 'How important … ' or 'How successfully … ' or 'How valid … ' part of the question. However, a basic analysis has been made.

Remember! To get a basic analysis comment mark you must make a simple comment that links to the subject of the question you are answering. Do it four times in your extended response and you can get up to four marks.

How do I gain extra marks for developed analysis?

Developed analysis or analysis plus will gain you a maximum of two more marks if you link your comments directly to the factor you are writing about.

In your introduction you included 'factors to develop'. In this topic on the New Deal the factors provided for you by the SQA are 'The first and second New Deals: the role of Roosevelt and "confidence building"; the role of the federal government; the economic effects of the New Deal.'

Assuming your extended responses are properly organised with separate paragraphs dealing with each factor, to get a developed analysis mark your comments must link to the factor you are writing about and not just generally to the topic of the essay. For example, if you were writing about FDR's closing of banks for three days (which is a Knowledge point) and you wrote 'The closing of the banks for three days was important because it helped restore confidence and helped the recovery of America under the New Deal' you will get a basic analysis mark because what you wrote is true but it only linked to the overall topic of the essay.

To get developed analysis marks, more focus is needed on the factor you are writing about, which in this case is 'the role of Roosevelt and "confidence building"'. So you should write something like:

Roosevelt's decision to close the banks for three days and carry out inspections was important because it helped restore confidence in banks as places to keep your money. Ordinary Americans felt confident enough to reinvest their savings thanks to Roosevelt's encouragement and action to ensure bank stability. This recovery of confidence in banks in turn provided funds for banks to invest in industry and so help the economy to recover.

Developed analysis marks are given for explaining why the factor you are writing about was more or less important than other factors in answering the question.

Another way to gain evaluation marks is to point out alternative interpretations of an action or event by comparing the opinions of other historians and making a decision, with reasons, why you think one opinion is more valid than another.

1–2 marks can be awarded for isolated evaluative comments used as a direct answer to the main question but 3–4 marks can be awarded where the candidate connects the evaluative comments together and links them to the line of argument outlined in the introduction.

The Civil Rights Movement – the prejudice continues

6

When the Second World War ended in 1945 little seemed to have changed for African-Americans. As the troop ships docked in US harbours, returning service men and women were told 'White troops to the right, niggers to the left.' Nevertheless, World War Two played a large part in laying the foundations of a more determined and focused civil rights campaign.

African-Americans had not benefited much from Roosevelt's New Deal. Unemployment had remained high throughout the 1930s and it was the boost given to the American economy by the demands for war production that finally brought prosperity back to the USA; yet most African-Americans did not see the change. As a result the African-American working class grew frustrated with their relative poverty during a time of recovering prosperity.

To quote from *Black, Brown and White*, a song recorded in 1939 by blues guitarist and singer Big Bill Broonzy:

> *Me and a man was workin' side by side*
> *This is what it meant*
> *They was paying him a dollar an hour*
> *And they was paying me fifty cent.*

When the USA entered the Second World War in 1942 there was great determination among many African-Americans that things had to change. Two months after the United States entered the war, the African-American *Pittsburgh Courier* newspaper announced a 'Double V' campaign for victory against fascism abroad and racism at home.

Across the country civil rights organisations fought racism and demanded equal access to New Deal social welfare benefits. In 1941, African-American leader A. Philip Randolph threatened to lead a movement of 100,000 people on a 'March on Washington' if employment in wartime production factories was not desegregated. President Roosevelt responded to the threat of disruption to production by signing Executive Order 8802. The order did not desegregate the defence industries fully but it did create a Fair Employment Practices Commission and was an early signal as to how vital federal and Presidential help would be in the future civil rights struggle.

Source 6.1

A political poster for the National Association for the Advancement of Colored People (NAACP).

How can you tell from the content of this poster that the campaign for civil rights was active during the Second World War? How does it illustrate both of the 'V' aims in the Double V campaign?

Meanwhile, civil rights campaigners continued to make the point that racism and disadvantaged ghettos were not only present in Nazi-occupied Europe – they existed in US cities also. As a sign of the growing organisation of African-American protest, James Farmer and Bayard Rustin helped form the Congress of Racial Equality (CORE) in 1942, which was to become a famous part of the struggle for civil rights in the 1950s and 1960s.

Before the Second World War racism had been widely accepted as a 'normal' feature of life in most Western nations, including the United States. After the Second World War the world had changed. From the late 1940s through to the 1960s, struggles of African and Asian people and the weakening of several European empires led to independence for 'non-white' countries. For African-Americans, the liberation struggles of black people abroad were both inspiring and frustrating. John Lewis later became a significant player in the civil rights campaign. He wrote:

> *They were getting their freedom, and we still didn't have ours in what we believed was a free country. We couldn't even get a hamburger and a Coke at the soda fountain.*

The Civil Rights Movement – the prejudice continues

Triggers, motivation and inspiration

In the mid 1950s three events happened which acted as catalysts, or triggers, that sparked off the civil rights campaigns that changed America. These events were:

   the Supreme Court decision of 1954;

   the murder of an African-American teenager named Emmett Till in 1955;

   the Montgomery Bus Boycott, also in 1955.

However, the events did not just happen in isolation. They were products of the wider context of change in the USA.

What was the importance of the Supreme Court decision of 1954?

In 1952, with the help of the NAACP, Oliver L. Brown from the city of Topeka, Kansas took the Topeka Board of Education to court over which school his daughter Linda could attend. Mr Brown was African-American and was supported in this action by the NAACP, who used the case of Linda Brown as an opportunity to attack segregation in education.

Remember! You should remember that in 1896 the Supreme Court had decided that segregation was acceptable as long as both white and non-white US citizens had 'separate but equal' facilities, which included schools.

Eventually, the case of '*Brown versus the Topeka Board of Education*' reached the Supreme Court and on Monday 17 May 1954 the Supreme Court declared:

> *In the field of public education the doctrine of 'separate but equal' has no place.*

In other words, the Supreme Court said the idea of 'separate but equal' had no place in modern America and that separating children in the schools because of the colour of their skin was wrong. The separate but equal decision of 1896 was completely reversed.

The decision of the Supreme Court was seen as a major turning point for civil rights and it was an inspirational moment; however, its immediate effect was limited. It was also a politically useful decision which must be seen in the light of the Cold War with the USSR (Russia). During this period the USA and the Soviet Union were competing for global influence, each side trying to show that its political system was the best. While Russia was the leader of the Communist World, the USA claimed it was the leader of the Free World. The USA held itself up as the land of the free. How could the USA claim that if children were banned from schools because of the colour of their skin?

In its 1954 ruling against school segregation, the Supreme Court agreed with the NAACP lawyers who argued that each and every decision regarding the lives of African-Americans could have consequences on the propaganda war between the USA and USSR. The Supreme Court stated that examples of racial discrimination within America were gifts to the propaganda machines of the Communist world and even friendly nations might start to wonder about the USA's genuine support for democracy and freedom.

Source 6.2

This newspaper front page is reporting on the Supreme Court decision of 1954. How does the report make clear its major importance but also its possible weakness? By using evidence from the front page, explain where most resistance to the Supreme Court's decision comes from and why.

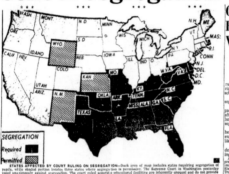

The 1954 Supreme Court decision that segregation in schools was unconstitutional had a huge impact on African-Americans. Change is always more likely when people realise that change **can** happen and is no longer just a hope. A door that is locked remains locked, but a door that is unlocked and slightly open is much easier to push wide open. However, there remained the problem of how to apply a federal decision on states who had their own rights over education. Although the Supreme Court decision marked an important change in attitudes towards segregation, it took many years to have much of an effect on Southern schools. Even ten years after the decision most school districts in the South continued to use some kind of educational segregation.

The murder of Emmett Till

In the mid-1950s an event happened that was, sadly, sickeningly normal. Emmett Till was a fourteen-year-old boy from Chicago who went to visit relatives near Money, Mississippi. An incident occurred in a local grocery store and three days later Emmett Till's body was found in the Tallahatchie River. One eye was gouged out, and his crushed-in head had a bullet in it.

There was a heavy engine tied around his neck with barbed wire. The corpse was almost unrecognisable.

The murder of Emmett Till itself was not that different from hundreds of previous murders, but what made the Till murder and trial different was the action of Emmett's mother. She insisted that her son was returned to Chicago and his mutilated body was displayed in a glass-topped coffin. Over four days, thousands of people saw Emmett's body. People who only a few years ago would never have heard of a murder in the South now had pictures of Emmett Till's battered body in national magazines and on national news reports on radio and television. New technology – the microphone and the TV film camera – turned a murder in a small town into a national anger that motivated so many people to become involved in the civil rights struggle.

Source 6.3

Why do you think the murder of Emmett Till had such an effect on attitudes towards racism in the South?

The Montgomery Bus Boycott

One of the most famous events in civil rights history is the Montgomery Bus Boycott. Rosa Parks was a middle-aged African-American who was tired after working a long day in a large downtown store and refused to give up her seat on a bus to a white passenger. She was arrested, a bus boycott started and after a time segregation on buses stopped. But why did the arrest of one woman lead to a massive campaign involving hundreds, if not thousands, of people? And did the bus boycott in one town really end segregation?

Rosa Parks was in no way the first, and certainly not the last, black citizen to resist Jim Crow laws in the South. The roots of the bus boycott began years before the arrest of Rosa Parks. The Women's Political Council (WPC), founded in 1946, was a group of African-American professionals who planned a boycott in 1955. To give their movement more focus, they needed a respected member of the community to be arrested for violating a city bus law. Rosa Parks had been a life-long worker for the NAACP, and as Martin Luther King wrote later, 'she was one of the most respected people in the Negro community'. From this point of view, Rosa Parks was a player in a much wider strategy, rather than a lone woman who was too tired to give up her seat on a bus.

Source 6.4

This is an example of a storyboard telling the story of the Montgomery Bus Boycott. What two things are done really well on the storyboard? Make one suggestion for an improvement.

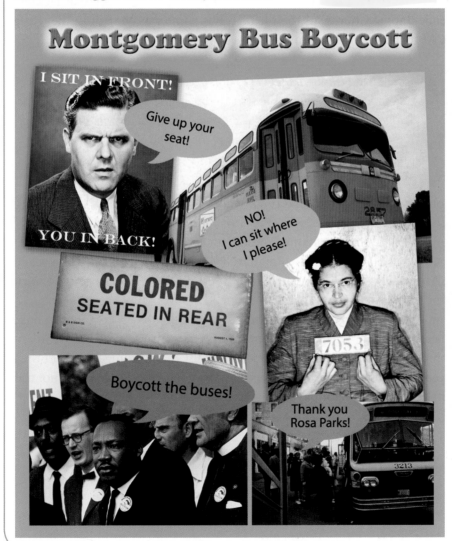

In Montgomery, Alabama, buses were segregated just like most other places in the South. Certain seats on a bus were reserved for white customers and other seats for African-American passengers. When white seats became full African-Americans could be asked to get up out of their seats to make way for white passengers.

On the day of her arrest Parks was seated in a seat for black Americans. A white man got on board and found that all the 'white' seats were full. The bus driver told four black Americans to move further down the bus. Three of them did as they were told, but Parks refused to give up her seat and was arrested.

On 5 December 1955 Rosa Parks was convicted for violating bus segregation laws. This was the signal for a one-day boycott of city buses in protest against the conviction of Parks, organised by the WPC in Montgomery. Those who had organised the one-day boycott created an organisation called the Montgomery Improvement Association (MIA) and chose a charismatic 26-year-old church minister, in his first job at Dexter Avenue Baptist Church, as their leader. His name was Martin Luther King, Jnr. At that meeting King inspired the community:

 I want it to be known that we're going to work with grim and bold determination to gain justice on the buses in this city. And we are not wrong … If we are wrong, the Supreme Court of this nation is wrong. If we are wrong, the Constitution of the United States is wrong. If we are wrong, God Almighty is wrong.

Though some wanted to end the boycott after just one day, the majority of the MIA wanted the boycott to continue. In fact, the boycott lasted over a year. Without sustained, united and consistent pressure in the face of personal hardship nothing would have been achieved, but for over a year the African-American community in Montgomery, Alabama refused to ride the buses. Bus passenger numbers dropped by over 90 per cent. After 13 months the boycott ended when the bus company desegregated its buses rather than face financial ruin. For the first time an African-American community discovered its economic power. By maintaining a boycott they forced those who supported segregation to change their policies, if not their attitudes, simply by not paying bus fares.

Source 6.5

Describe how this poster captures the immediacy of direct action and the aims and methods of the protest.

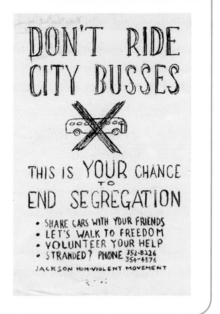

Was the Montgomery Bus Boycott important to the campaign for civil rights?

The Montgomery Bus Boycott had effects far beyond the story of buses in Montgomery. The actions and organisations of groups such as the MIO inspired other campaigns and individuals were motivated to take direct action to improve their lives. The boycott created a new leader in Martin Luther King, Jnr. The bus boycott showed that united, non-violent mass protest could successfully challenge racial segregation and was an example for other Southern campaigns that followed. On 10–11 January 1956, in Atlanta ministers in MIA met other ministers who worked in the South. The result of this meeting was the founding of the Southern Christian Leadership Conference.

However, immediate successes were limited. Segregation across the South did not collapse, Rosa Parks was forced to leave Montgomery due to death threats and if you were African-American it was virtually impossible to find any job in Montgomery. Regrettably, it was reported in 1963 that most African-Americans had returned to the old practice of riding in the back of the bus.

Why are the events at Little Rock in 1957 important to the story of civil rights?

Despite the decision of the Supreme Court in 1954 – that schools should be desegregated – most schools in the South remained unchanged. In 1957, at a school in Little Rock, Arkansas, nine African-American children tried to attend the white Central High School. Why did this event become such a huge milestone in civil rights and why did it gain such importance in the world?

First of all, what happened at Little Rock in 1957 led to a struggle between state power and federal power. The showdown at Little Rock involved a state governor, Orval Faubus, and the President of the USA, Dwight D. Eisenhower.

Secondly, television was a new technology in the 1950s and for the first time brought world issues into people's living rooms. Many Americans were shocked by what they saw of racism in the segregated South.

Finally, President Eisenhower was aware that the enemies of America were using the story of Little Rock to make the USA look bad in the eyes of the world. Eisenhower said:

 Our enemies are gloating over this incident and using it everywhere to misrepresent our whole nation.

The events at Little Rock were part of a strategy by the NAACP to force the schools to desegregate and accept the 1954 decision of the Supreme Court. The nine students selected to enter Central High School were recruited by Daisy Bates, president of the Arkansas branch of the NAACP. They were also all high-achievers so that there could be no complaints that the African-Americans were lowering standards in Central High School.

On the day before the African-American students were due to attend Little Rock High School, the NAACP decided to postpone the actions in the face of violent crowd demonstrations. Unfortunately, one student, 15-year-old Elizabeth Eckford, was not told about the change of plan and here is her account of what happened:

 The crowd moved closer and closer. I looked into the face of an old woman and she spat on me. The crowd moved closer and closer. Somebody started yelling, 'Lynch her! Lynch her! No nigger bitch is going to get in our school. Get out of here!' Someone hollered, 'Drag her over to this tree! Let's take care of that nigger.'

Pictures and film of the events at Little Rock made national and international headlines. Russia used the images to claim that America was very far from being a land of the free. President Eisenhower realised the international damage that was being done to the image of the USA around the world. He said:

 At a time when we face grave situations abroad because of the hatred that communism bears towards a system of government based on human rights, it would be difficult to exaggerate the harm that is being done to the prestige and influence and indeed to the safety of our nation and the world by images from Little Rock.

Source 6.6

Does this book cover illustrate successfully the events and issues involved in the crisis at Little Rock High School in 1957?

Something had to be done. But did the President take action to help African-American students because it was the right thing to do or because it was politically useful to do so?

Eisenhower was well aware that his Presidential authority was being challenged by Governor Orval Faubus. Faubus had called out the Arkansas National Guard, claiming that they were deployed around Little Rock to maintain law and order. In reality they were stopping any African-American student from entering the Central High School.

What was President Eisenhower to do? Eisenhower had publicly stated only two months earlier that he would not use federal troops to support the African-American community in the South, simply because he believed that laws could not change what was in people's heads and hearts. But the President was no longer willing to have individual states in the USA ignoring federal law. Nor was he prepared to allow America to be criticised by its enemies around the world.

Eisenhower spent 18 days negotiating with Faubus. During this time, the African-American students stayed at home and the school remained guarded by the National Guard. They only left the school when a federal court ordered them to leave.

When Faubus took away the National Guardsmen there was now nothing to stop the mob from attacking any African-American students near Central High School. President Eisenhower took action. He sent one thousand US paratroopers into Arkansas and for the first time in a hundred years the federal government had used force to help the African-American community.

Source 6.7

How does this cartoon from 1957 simply sum up the issues surrounding the Little Rock Crisis?

Compare this image with the one on p.103. Which one do you prefer as informative evidence about the Little Rock Crisis?

The events at Little Rock in 1957 reminded the Northern states and the rest of the world that racism still existed in the South, while the African-American community was also inspired and encouraged by the sight of US troops being used to protect their rights. On the other hand, Governor Faubus was re-elected as governor of Arkansas and rather than desegregate his schools he closed them! Little Rock Central High School did not open up with a desegregated school population until 1960. As late as 1964, only three per cent of African-American school children attended desegregated schools.

Direct action

By the late 1950s the actions of the NAACP in pushing for change through the law courts and the direct action of African-Americans no longer prepared to put up with the racism of white authorities led to more actions challenging segregation. Those young, media-savvy campaigners were now well aware of the power of film cameras and microphones to gain huge sympathy and support from around the world. It was hoped direct action would create pressure for federal action to enforce integration. New and not-so-new organisations became involved in direct action and all adopted peaceful, non-violent tactics while displaying civil disobedience, as explained and demonstrated by Martin Luther King.

Martin Luther King followed the teachings of Mahatma Gandhi, who had used civil disobedience and non-violent protest in his struggles for Indian independence from Britain in the 1940s. King had grown up in Atlanta and witnessed segregation and racism every day. He was 'fascinated by the idea of refusing to co-operate with an evil system' as he wrote in *Stride Toward Freedom* in 1958. His belief in civil disobedience was founded on the idea of just and unjust laws. As he wrote:

> *One has not only a legal, but a moral responsibility to obey just laws. Conversely, one has a moral responsibility to disobey unjust laws.*
>
> Martin Luther King, Jnr, Letter from Birmingham Jail

King also explained his belief in non-violent protest: 'Nonviolence is a powerful and just weapon which cuts without wounding and ennobles the man who wields it.' King spoke with authority and dignity. In a few short years he had become the media front man of the civil rights campaign. Many others worked with King – for example, Ralph Abernathy of SCLC and John Lewis of SNCC – but King was the 'face, the voice and the inspiration of the campaign'.

The focus of attention now turned to the actions of black and white students, who put new life into the Civil Rights Movement through a series of sit-ins. A sit-in or sit-down protest is defined as a form of direct action that involves one or more people occupying an area for a protest often to promote political or social change. It is a non-violent way to effectually shut down an area or business. The forced removal of protesters, and sometimes the use of violence against them, gains publicity, often arouses sympathy and usually leads to success.

In the case of protests against segregation, the Congress of Racial Equality (CORE) had conducted sit-ins during the 1940s but the most famous sit-in of the civil rights campaign began in the late 1950s and involved not only CORE but a new organisation of students – the SNCC.

African-American students had created the SNCC in April 1960 to help co-ordinate, support and publicise the sit-in campaign. SNCC stood for Student Non-violent Coordinating Committee and their first target was segregated lunch counters across the South. The students of SNCC were well organised and well prepared. In Nashville, Tennessee the students formed the Nashville Student Movement and were trained by civil rights activist Jim Lawson. In Lawson's classes students took part in protest workshops and roleplay, preparing for the day they would be assaulted and insulted yet remain non-violent. Lawson was a member of CORE but his training of groups in the tactics of nonviolence was carried out on behalf of the SCLC. Once again, tactics, organisation and leadership were seen as vital ingredients to success.

Sit-ins targeted lunch counters like fast-food cafés with a counter where food was served. At the counters there were stools for white customers only to sit on. Joseph McNeil was involved in the most famous of the sit-ins in Greensboro, North Carolina and describes the tactics of the protest:

> We sat at a lunch counter where blacks never sat before. We asked for service, and we were denied, and we expected to be denied. We asked why couldn't we be served. It was our intent to sit there until they decided to serve us.

McNeil and three others remained in their seats until closing. They returned the following day with 25 supporters who continued the 'sit-in'. By 5 February there were more than 300 students, black and white, taking part in the protest.

TV news showed local white youths attacking the demonstrator, but when the police arrived it was the demonstrators who were arrested. The problem was that as soon as demonstrators were carried away from the lunch counters more demonstrators took their place. The police, the jails and the courts all over the South were being overwhelmed by the campaign to 'fill the jails'. By doing this the protestors were creating huge headaches for local authorities. How were so many people in local jails to be fed? Kept healthy? How were other court cases to be heard?

Although thousands of the students were arrested and physically assaulted, they refused to retaliate. The campaign methods of the students is a good example of civil disobedience and non-violent protest.

Source 6.8

What is the significance of the photograph and the words in this image. How do they relate to the direct action of SNCC in 1960?

The sit-ins at a Woolworth's store in Greensboro, North Carolina, launched a wave of anti-segregation sit-ins across the South. The publicity surrounding the sit-ins achieved not only desegregation at some lunch counters but more importantly they increased national awareness of the depth of segregation in the South. In a very real sense the sit-ins were a training ground for student activists who went on to lead, plan and direct almost every part of the Civil Rights Movement in the 1960s. However, the protests only hardened attitudes among white segregationists in the South.

Sit-ins had exposed and challenged yet more examples of segregation in the South. The success of direct action such as sit-ins encouraged CORE activists to organise a new risky strategy to challenge segregation. The first Freedom Ride took place in 1961.

What were the Freedom Rides?

In 1960 a Supreme Court decision had banned segregation in public areas, such as waiting rooms and restaurants, for travellers using buses that went from one state to another. Interstate highways (like motorways) and the service area restrooms were the responsibility of the national federal authority, not state authority. In areas under federal authority there should have been no segregation. In 1961 a group of black and white members of CORE planned to travel south on interstate buses. They became known as Freedom Riders.

In May 1961, thirteen members of CORE rode from Washington to New Orleans in the Southern state of Mississippi. They wanted to test if segregation in interstate public facilities had really ended. Members of SNCC also joined the Freedom Rides.

Source 6.9

What is the significance of the photograph and the words in this image. How do they relate to the direct action of CORE in 1961?

The group encountered tremendous violence from white protestors along the route and TV news coverage of the attacks on the Freedom Riders deeply shocked the American public. As James Farmer, a main organiser of the Freedom Rides, wrote about his experiences on the Freedom Rides:

 I was certain I was going to die. What kind of death would it be? Well, damn it, if I had to die, I hoped the newspapers were out there. Plenty of them. With plenty of cameras.

How important were the Freedom Rides?

The freedom rides, like the sit-ins before them, demonstrated that anyone who opposed segregation could take action themselves to work towards ending Jim Crow laws. On the other hand, there is a view that the Freedom Rides did little to change the real problem, which was that black Americans had little power themselves to change the way the country was run. As James M. Lawson, writing in the *Southern Patriot* newspaper reported in 1961:

> *It would be well to recognize that we have been receiving concessions, not real changes. The sit-ins won concessions, not structural changes; the Freedom Rides won great concessions, but not real change. Remember that the way to get this revolution off the ground is to forge pressure which the President cannot ignore.*

The message of Lawson was not lost on the protesters, who had marched and campaigned for many years. Questions were being asked within the Civil Rights Movement about King's leadership, the non-violent strategy and the discontent of protesters, who were being arrested, losing wages and perhaps jobs and all for what? Was anything significant really going to change regarding civil rights? In December 1961, Martin Luther King and the SCLC became involved in a campaign in Albany, Georgia, which proved to be a serious problem for the civil rights campaign.

As students of history, we know the basic story of what happened in the civil rights campaign. With hindsight, we know that significant civil rights victories were won. For African-Americans in the early 1960s, it was sometimes difficult to see how much progress was actually being made and success was by no means guaranteed.

By 1962 the Civil Rights Movement was in trouble. The protests so far had made white authorities make some changes but they were localised. As John Lewis observed, the sit-ins, boycotts and freedom rides had won *concessions* but not rights. A concession is something granted as a favour or gesture but which is not mandatory. Rights, on the other hand, mean *legal* entitlement – a RIGHT to equality as American citizens enshrined in law. Supreme Court rulings concerning the constitutional rights of African-Americans were still being ignored and many campaigners began to question where the movement was heading. Federal government still did not support the campaign and KKK violence was as brutal as ever. For several years protestors had been arrested, lost income and jobs and faced violent attack, but for what?

The campaign organised by SNCC students in Albany against segregation encountered problems from the start, particularly as the they received no support from the NAACP, who were perhaps jealous of the headline-

grabbing tactics of the SNCC's Freedom Riders. Meanwhile, SNCC local activists were angered when Martin Luther King arrived in the area. The SNCC had wanted a local campaign led by local leaders over local issues.

When the campaign started it was clear the local authorities had learned lessons from the previous campaigns. Those earlier campaigns were successful primarily when they were given publicity. Media coverage gained sympathy across the USA and forced federal government to take notice. In Albany, the local authorities avoided such mistakes. They decided students would be arrested but then released. In this way, there would be no confrontation and the nation's media would be starved of images to fill newspapers and televisions news. The lack of violence also meant that the federal government had no reason to intervene.

Finally, the local authorities in Albany promised to meet protestors demands yet delivered little. They realised that promises could be easily broken as soon as the demonstrators moved out of town! When King left Albany the protests fizzled out. The Albany local authority brazenly broke their promises: city parks were closed, swimming pools were shut down and schools remained segregated. The Albany protest also illustrated the lack of cooperation between the SNCC, SCLC and the NAACP.

Support for the protests began to dwindle. Albany was recognised as a major defeat by the Civil Rights Movement, but King had also learned lessons: that local authorities could *break* as well as make promises. In the past, success had been won through a combination of widespread media coverage and economic pressure. If local businesses were losing money because of segregation, then segregation would surely go! The focus, therefore, turned on Birmingham, Alabama.

Birmingham, 1963

Protesting in Birmingham, Alabama would be a high-risk strategy, but King believed a campaign in the city would get the Civil Rights Movement back on track. A campaign in Birmingham offered King some advantages. The plan called for direct non-violent action to attract media attention to 'the biggest and baddest city of the South'.

Firstly, both SNCC and the NAACP were not heavily involved in the area so King could lead a SCLC campaign without too much competition against what he called 'the most segregated city in the United States'. Secondly, King knew that any civil rights campaign in Birmingham would almost certainly provoke trouble and gain the movement national publicity, which would in turn provoke the federal government to take action.

The planned demonstrations in Birmingham were known as Project C. The 'C' stood for confrontation. King had summarised the philosophy of the Birmingham campaign when he said: 'The purpose of ... direct action is to

create a situation so crisis-packed that it will inevitably open the door to negotiation.' King and his follow demonstrators knew that local police chief Eugene 'Bull' Connor had a short temper and was easily provoked into extreme, even insane, actions.

King's strategy of civil disobedience depended on large numbers of protestors who were prepared to break the law and risk going to jail. However, in the first few days of the campaign, not enough people were arrested to affect the functioning of the city. The campaign was losing momentum; King wondered what he should do. He knew he was the face and the voice of the campaign and his services as a fundraiser were desperately needed. However, King was also worried that his failure to submit to arrest might undermine his credibility. King concluded that he must risk going to jail in Birmingham. The next day, 12 April 1963, King marched and was arrested for the thirteenth time.

King was kept in solitary confinement and was refused the right to see his lawyer. In prison he wrote a stirring *Letter From Birmingham Jail* in which he eloquently argued against those who disliked his methods and urged him to wait for change. He replied:

> *For years now I have heard the word 'Wait!' ... I guess it is easy for those who have never seen vicious mobs lynch your fathers and mothers and drown your brothers and sisters ... when your tongue becomes twisted as you try to explain to your six-year-old daughter why she can't go to the amusement park advertised on TV and see the tears welling up in her little eyes when you tell her that Funtown is closed to colored children ... then you will know why it is difficult to wait.*
>
> *Martin Luther King, Jnr*, Letter from Birmingham Jail

Meanwhile, events outside prison were taking the Birmingham campaign in a new direction. It was while King was in prison that SCLC's Director of Direct Action, James Bevell, realised young African-American students were an untapped source of freedom fighters. They did not risk losing jobs and they had no income to lose while in jail. Bevell's plan was later called the 'Children's Crusade' by *Newsweek* magazine. It was a high-risk strategy, but on 2 May more than a thousand students skipped school and gathered at the 16th Street Baptist Church. As they marched, more than 600 students were arrested. The youngest of those arrested was eight years old. By 6 May the jails were so full that Connor used the grounds of a local fairground as a temporary jail to hold protesters. It took four hours to feed the prisoners with breakfast! More importantly, the 'Children's Crusade' received front-page coverage in the *Washington Post* and the *New York Times*.

At this point Bull Connor delivered the publicity that the campaigners had wanted. On 7 May Connor ordered the city's fire hoses, set at a level that would peel bark off a tree, to be turned on the children. He also ordered police attack dogs to be set on marching school children! Suddenly Birmingham got national attention. Television cameras broadcast to the nation and American people watched in shock and disbelief as white police officers attacked school children, first with powerful fire hoses and then with tear gas, dogs and electric cattle prods.

Source 6.10 and 6.11

Why were photographs like the 'firehose' and 'dogs' so important to the Civil Rights Movement? Do the photographs prove that the Civil Rights Movement was carefully organised and disciplined?

President John F. Kennedy later said of 'Bull' Connor, 'The Civil Rights Movement should thank God for Bull Connor. He's helped it as much as Abraham Lincoln.' As a result of the publicity surrounding the Children's Crusade, national pressure on President Kennedy was increasing. Birmingham's own business community was also desperate for a solution. Their trade had collapsed and the bad publicity that Birmingham was getting on national TV was likely to damage their businesses for a long time. Negotiations between African-American leaders of the Birmingham community and representatives of Birmingham's city's business leadership were held and on 10 May negotiators reached an agreement often called 'The Birmingham Truce Agreement'. The details of the compromise included the removal of 'Whites Only' and 'Blacks Only' signs in restrooms and on drinking fountains as well as a plan to desegregate lunch counters.

The truce was short-lived. Only the day after the compromise was reached an explosion went off near the Gaston Motel where King and SCLC leaders had previously stayed. When more police arrived a riot broke out, numerous buildings and vehicles were burned and several people, including a police officer, were stabbed.

Kennedy was moved to take action in much the same way that Eisenhower and Roosevelt had been forced into action. Public sympathy and support for civil rights was high and Kennedy could not ignore the mood of the public. Kennedy was also very aware of the international embarrassment that the Birmingham demonstrations were causing. The Soviet Union devoted up to 25 per cent of its news broadcast to the demonstrations, sending much of it to Africa, where Soviet and US interests were in competition for influence.

Kennedy ordered an end to segregation in Birmingham. By 13 May three thousand federal troops were on the streets of Birmingham to restore order. Kennedy had also realised that only federal action and federal law could stop the violence that had sparked off in Birmingham from spreading across the USA.

As a result of these pressures, Kennedy appeared on television on 11 June and promised action based on the principle that:

… race has no place in American society. The events in Birmingham and elsewhere have so increased cries for equality that [we cannot] choose to ignore them. I am, therefore, asking the Congress to enact legislation [to pass a law] giving all Americans the right to be served in facilities which are open to the public. I am also asking Congress … to end segregation in public schools.

It looked as if President Kennedy had been convinced that the federal government of the USA should make a new Civil Rights Law – but would it really happen? What could be done now to make sure that the federal government kept its promise? In the 1940s A. Philip Randolph had suggested a march on Washington in an attempt to force the US Government to improve civil rights. In the summer of 1963 the time seemed right to carry out a new March for Jobs and Freedom.

On 28 August over 200,000 people of mixed races marched towards the Lincoln Memorial in Washington D.C. It was the largest civil rights demonstration in American history and four national television channels broadcast the event live. The speech Martin Luther King gave has become known as the 'I have a dream' speech and is considered to be one of the most famous and important speeches of the twentieth century.

Source 6.12

March on Washington for Jobs and Freedom.

Source 6.13

How does the lapel badge from 1963 (Source 6.12) and this 50th anniversary poster illustrate the aims, methods, leadership and most famous event of the March on Washington?

The March on Washington put the Civil Rights Movement back in the headlines, but when President Kennedy was assassinated in November 1963, it looked like the movement had gained nothing. However, incoming President Lyndon Johnson made sure that the Civil Rights Act became law. Years of protests had eventually resulted in the 1964 Civil Rights Act.

What did the Civil Rights Act of 1964 do?

The Civil Rights Act applied to the entire nation, prohibiting racial discrimination in employment and in access to public places. It made discrimination and segregation based on skin colour or race illegal. Discrimination on the basis of race in any or all public places in the USA was banned. This included petrol stations, restaurants, hotels, movie theatres and airline terminals. The only exceptions were places that served fewer than five people. There were also to be equal opportunities in the workplace. It became unlawful for a business employing more than 25 people to discriminate on the basis of 'race, national origin, religion, or gender'. The federal Justice Department was allowed to take to court any state government that still discriminated against African-Americans.

For many Americans, the Civil Rights Act of 1964 was a big move towards helping African-Americans achieve full civil rights, but Martin Luther King and others argued that only way to get real change was to get the right to vote without restrictions. He said that the new Civil Rights Act law gave Negroes 'some part of their rightful dignity, but without the vote it was dignity without strength'.

The problem was that very few African-Americans were registered to vote. In the USA any adult who wants to vote must first of all register to vote. African-Americans had been given the right to vote in 1870, but in the years that followed, Southern states had made it more and more difficult for African-Americans to register to vote. King believed that 'the denial of the right to vote was the very origin, the root cause, of racial segregation in the South'.

By the early 1960s it was still difficult for African-Americans to register to vote. Registration officials used such tactics as restricting opening hours when registration could take place and those who tried to register were threatened with losing their jobs or their homes, boycotts of their businesses and even threats to their lives. This obstruction of voter registration worked. In 1961, in Dallas County, Alabama, out of 15,000 African-Americans old enough to vote, only 130 were registered. That was less than one per cent of possible voters.

Civil rights campaigners looked at the success of Birmingham and knew that part of the success was due to violent white resistance, which had

gained publicity and support for the Civil Rights Movement. A similar potential for grabbing media attention existed around the city of Selma, the main town in Dallas County, Alabama. The Governor of Alabama, George Wallace, had promised 'Segregation forever!' and the Sheriff of Dallas County, Jim Clark, was also known to be very like Bull Connor in his attitudes and speed of losing his temper!

Organisers from the SNCC began working on efforts to register black voters as part of the growing civil rights campaign of the early 1960s, but progress was slow. Local officials continued to obstruct attempts by the African-American community to register for the vote. Overall more than 3000 people were arrested in protests between 1 January and 7 February, but only 100 more African-Americans had managed to register for the vote. When one of the campaigners, Jimmie Lee Jackson, was shot dead by a police officer, SNCC workers requested help from Martin Luther King, Jnr and the activists of the SCLC.

King told his staff, 'we need to make a dramatic appeal because the people of Selma are tired'. King might well have added that the people of Selma were resigned to reality. By the end of February 1965, only 300 African-Americans were registered in Selma, compared to 9500 whites. What could King do to force change?

King informed the President on 9 February of his decision to use Selma, Alabama as a centre for a series of protest marches. Against King stood Governor Wallace who stated: 'There will be no marches between Selma and Montgomery.' Governor Wallace denounced the marches as a threat to public safety and said that he would take all measures necessary to prevent them from happening. Wallace also ordered Alabama Highway Patrol Chief Al Lingo to 'use whatever measures are necessary to prevent a march'.

King set the scene for further confrontation by gaining maximum publicity. On 1 February 1965, over a month before the march was due to take place, Martin Luther King got himself arrested quite deliberately. After all, he had just gained worldwide fame as the winner of the Nobel Peace Prize, a world famous award. King was on the front cover of almost every magazine and newspaper. He was on TV news and chat shows almost every night. The face of Martin Luther King was iconic and he had no problem with using his fame to increase pressure for change.

King's arrest was, therefore, big news and it is now clear that this was a publicity stunt. Before he was arrested, King and others in the SCLC had prepared a speech that would be sent to newspapers when King was in jail. On 5 February the *New York Times* printed the speech:

" *Why are we in jail? When the Civil Rights Act of 1964 was passed many decent Americans thought the day of difficult struggle was over. By jailing hundreds of Negroes the city of Selma, Alabama has revealed the persisting ugliness of segregation. There are more Negroes in jail with me than there are on the voting registers. This is the USA in 1965. We are in jail because we cannot tolerate these conditions for our nation.*

The first protest march was planned for 7 March 1965 between Selma and Montgomery. On that day about 600 civil rights marchers left Selma. They walked peacefully and did not interfere with traffic. The march was led by John Lewis of SNCC and the Reverend Hosea Williams of SCLC. The protest went according to plan until the marchers tried to cross the Edmund Pettus Bridge into Dallas County.

Source 6.14

Waiting for the marchers were about 200 state troopers and local police mounted on horseback. The police were all armed with tear gas, sticks and bull whips. The marchers were ordered to turn back but seconds later they began shoving the demonstrators, knocking many to the ground and beating them with police batons. Another group of troopers fired tear gas while mounted troopers charged the crowd on horseback.

Televised images of the brutal attack presented Americans and international audiences with horrifying images of marchers left bloodied and severely injured, and this roused support for the Selma Voting Rights Campaign. George B. Leonard wrote in *The Nation* on 10 May 1965:

> *There are moments when outrage turns to action. One of these moments came, not on Sunday, March 7, when a group of Negroes at Selma were gassed, clubbed and trampled by horses, but on the following day when films of the event appeared on national television.*

Source 6.15

Can you, with confidence and detail, explain the connection between Sources 6.14 and 6.15, one depicting orderly, peaceful protestors crossing the Edmund Pettus Bridge and the other showing police wearing gas masks, beating the marchers?

On the surface it seemed that the Civil Rights Movement and most of the USA stood united in the face of racist aggression but within the movement something odd happened.

You may already have read that divisions within the Civil Rights Movement had existed during the March on Washington, while at the Birmingham demonstrations there were some leaders who were less than happy with King's non-violent approach. Tensions also existed between the more non-violent SCLC and the increasingly radical SNCC. When King reached the Birmingham Compromise some civil rights leaders accused King of being too concerned with pleasing the white American population.

The claim that King was too soft on his opposition gained more supporters during the second Selma march. Two days after the attack on the Edmund Pettus Bridge, Martin Luther King led about 2500 marchers out on the Edmund Pettus Bridge, held a short prayer session then turned back without confronting the police. It soon became clear that King had done a deal with the Selma authorities including Lingo and Sheriff Clark. They had agreed a route on which King was allowed to march so that a court order banning marches was not broken. Only SCLC leaders had been told in advance of the plan, and many marchers felt confused and angered by King's 'Turnaround

Tuesday'. Hundreds of marchers had travelled long distances to take part and oppose police brutality. Now they had lost their opportunity.

Dr King's credibility in the Civil Rights Movement was shaken by the secret turnaround agreement and SNCC members were eager to break away from King's strategy of civil disobedience and non-violent protest.

Eventually Martin Luther King and his supporters gained legal permission to march from Selma to Montgomery. On 21 March the march began again. This time US troops and FBI agents protected the marchers. At the end of the Selma to Montgomery march on 25 March 1965 King spoke to the 25,000 other marchers and once again made it clear what the purpose of the civil rights campaign was:

 America's conscience has been sleeping but now it is waking up.
Let us march on segregated housing . . .
Let us march on segregated schools . . .
Let us march on poverty . . .
Let us march on ballot boxes . . .
Let us march on to the American Dream.

The marches had a powerful effect in Washington. The third march received national and international coverage but even before the march, President Johnson had presented a Voting Rights Bill to Congress. Johnson also spoke on national television. He said:

 What happened in Selma is part of a far larger movement which reaches into every section and state of America. It is the effort of American Negroes to secure for themselves the full blessings of American life. Their cause must be our cause ... And we shall overcome.

Many in the Civil Rights Movement were astonished by the speech. After so long, and so hard a struggle, finally a President was willing to defend voting rights for African-Americans. According to C.T. Vivian, an SCLC activist, the speech was 'a victory like none other. It was an affirmation of our movement'. However, other campaigners were much more cynical. They argued Johnson had no alternative, given the international scandal caused by the police at the Edmund Pettus Bridge. The USA was also involved in an expensive war in Vietnam, fighting for 'freedom' against communism. In the frontline were thousands of African-American soldiers. Could they look forward to freedom in their homeland?

On 6 August 1965, Lyndon B. Johnson signed the Voting Rights Act. Individual states lost their right to restrict who could vote. Johnson

President Johnson had suspected for a long time that a minority of people were using the urban problems as a means of starting a revolution in America. He did not believe the riots were a genuine reaction of people who felt they had no other options but to use violence so he asked Otto Kerner, who was then governor of the state of Illinois, to investigate thoroughly the causes of the urban riots. The task of the Kerner Commission was to investigate the real causes of the urban riots based around three questions asked by the President:

- What happened?
- Why did it happen?
- What can be done to prevent it from happening again and again?

How effectively had the Civil Rights Movement, including the black radical groups, improved the lives of African-Americans by 1968?

When the Kerner Commission made its report public in 1968, Americans were shocked by what it said:

- America was divided into two societies – one black and poor, the other white and richer.
- 40 per cent of all black Americans lived in poverty.
- Black men were twice as likely to be unemployed as white men.
- Black men were three times as likely to be in low-skilled jobs.
- The riots and other crimes were caused by poverty.

The Kerner Commission concluded that 'our nation is moving towards two societies, one black, one white – separate and unequal'. It went on to say that:

> *White Americans have never understood – but what the Negro can never forget – is that white society is deeply implicated in the ghetto. White institutions created it, white institutions maintain it, and white society condones it.*

In other words, the problems of the urban ghettos were not caused by outside troublemakers. The problems of the ghettos were caused by genuine poverty resulting from the lack of opportunities for African-Americans to improve their lives.

President Johnson did not like what he read and ignored the report.

Source 7.11

Why did the Kerner Report deliberately contain the last three words used in this extract from the report?

How did the Report make the USA very uncomfortable about the progress that was thought to have been made in civil rights in the decades before 1968?

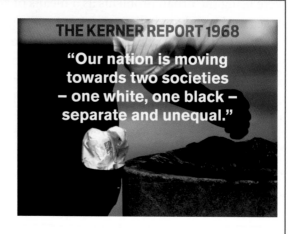

THE KERNER REPORT 1968

"Our nation is moving towards two societies – one white, one black – separate and unequal."

The civil rights campaign had led to great improvements in lives of African-Americans, especially in the South. Although attitudes could not change overnight, segregation and discrimination were now unlawful and federal law protected African-Americans.

Socially, the 1970s mainstream media made new African-American stars and peak-time programmes featuring almost entirely African-American casts. Politically, the election of African-American state officials, state representatives and Senators showed considerable political progress, finally reaching its peak with the election of Barack Obama as President in 2008.

However, for many poor African-Americans life remained difficult. The Kerner Commission reminded America that it was still a long way from being a free and equal society. The world was reminded of the civil rights issue at the 1968 Mexico Olympics when two African-American runners mounted the rostrum to receive their medals. As the Stars and Stripes flag rose and the American national anthem played, the athletes raised clenched fist salutes and bowed their heads. The world could see that Black Power was still alive in the United States and that racial tension still existed.

In fact, to mark the thirtieth anniversary of the Kerner Report, a new report was issued called *The Millennium Breach*. It reported:

 Today, thirty years after the Kerner Report, there is more poverty in America, it is deeper, blacker and browner than before, and it is more concentrated in the cities, which have become America's poorhouses.

Is it yet possible to say that black Americans are indeed 'Free at Last'?

Activities

1 If this is the answer what is the question?

Below you will find a list of words or names. You have to make up a question that can only be answered by the word on the list. For example, if the words 'Mexico Olympics' were the answer, a question could be 'Where did American athletes use Black Power salutes?' Here is your list of answers:

- Stokely Carmichael
- Nation of Islam
- Black Power
- Malcolm X
- Black Panthers
- Ghetto cycle of deprivation
- The Kerner Commission
- 4 April 1968

2 How far can you go?

Each set of two questions increases in difficulty. The first two are straightforward describe-and-explain questions. The final few questions require you to think quite hard about the chapter you have read. It is your choice where you stop.

a) Explain why the syllabus for this course uses the phrase 'resultant black radical groups'?

b) How did supporters of Black Power show their support of the movement?

c) How would you summarise the feelings of young African-Americans living in urban ghettos to the Civil Rights Act of 1964 and the Voting Rights Act of 1965?

d) Can you explain why support for the Civil Rights Movement faded away after 1965?

e) What are your thoughts on the effectiveness of images of Black Panthers used in both 'for' and 'against' media? Think of the positive as well as the negative reactions to the images.

f) If you had been a government adviser to President Johnson in 1968, how would you have advised him to react to the different but mounting pressures on the President at that time?

3 Question time

Work in pairs. In this activity make up at least ten questions that you would use to test someone's knowledge and understanding about the black radical groups in the 1960s.

continued

Activities continued

To make up the questions, first of all decide what you want the person to know about or what you want to find out about. You must have a clear idea of what answer you want for your question.

- This activity is different from previous tasks that asked about understanding. Those tasks included lots of 'Explain' questions.

- This activity is to check knowledge of facts. Questions that start with 'Who was' or 'Describe' or 'How did' are all suitable.

- Try to make up a mixture of big and small questions. A big question could be 'How did the black radical groups differ from the groups who followed Martin Luther King?' and a small question could be 'What organisation did Malcolm X represent before he left it?'

- You can arrange for questions to be spoken or written down, but in both cases answers should be presented as proper sentences.

- Your questions should be mature and well presented. The purpose is to help learning, not to catch people out with tricky, obscure facts.

When you have completed your ten questions try them out on each other. Can your partner answer your question? Can you answer your partner's question? Can you each make up five new questions based on information your partner did not know?

4 Revolving circle

Write a paragraph of between 100 and 200 words explaining the impact of increasingly violent civil rights protest in the 1960s.

Divide the class into two groups and form each group into a circle. One group makes an inner circle, the other makes the outer circle. You should face each other. Stand opposite a classmate.

Take it in turns to exchange information with each other for approximately one minute. Give your classmates a red, amber or green rating and at least one suggestion that they could have done in their presentation. The inner circle then rotates clockwise and the outer circle rotates anti-clockwise. The new pair repeats the process.

The rotation continues until you have all had the opportunity to share information with at least two classmates.

Unit assessment practice

Complete a unit assessment standard:

> European and World Outcome 2 asks you to draw on and apply knowledge and understanding of complex European and World historical issues in a number of ways.

> Assessment standard 2.3 asks you to analyse a European and World historical issue. An example might be:

Analyse the factors which were important in causing the rise of black radical movements in the 1960s.

Extended response practice and Top Tip 6: How to write a good conclusion

This top tip provides advice on how to write a good conclusion. The first thing to remember is that your essay or extended response **must** have a conclusion. For your extended response (essay) there are 4 available marks for structure. You can gain 2 out of these 4 marks for your conclusion. Don't dismiss 2 marks as unimportant. Two marks is the difference between a lower grade and a higher one and the 4 marks for structure could be the difference between a band C and a band A.

The examples provided here all relate to the SQA mandatory content topic:

> 'An assessment of the effectiveness of the Civil Rights Movement in meeting the needs of black Americans, up to 1968'.

What sort of question will I be asked?

When you are preparing for the exam think very carefully about the style of question you will be asked and what the question will be about. In this case **all** the extended response questions will be about the issue mentioned above. In simple English the issue means – 'Did the Civil Rights Movement really improve the lives of black Americans up to 1968?'

In this section you are asked to evaluate – or judge – how important the Civil Rights Movement was in improving the lives of black Americans up to 1968. Just as in the previous sections, the SQA provides illustrative examples of reasons to use in this section. For this section those illustrative examples are:

> the aims of the Civil Rights Movement and the roles of NAACP, CORE, SCLC and Martin Luther King in desegregation – methods and tactics;

> changes in federal policy;

> social, economic and political changes;

> the resultant rise of black radical movements.

There is no one correct answer in judging the effectiveness of the Civil Rights Movement so a marker is looking for you to use all the relevant illustrative examples in reaching your conclusion. You should also know about the style of question you will be asked and in this section you can be asked the 'how successful' question because the section is about judging the effectiveness of the Civil Rights Movement.

Examples of questions on this section could be:

1 To what extent were the methods and tactics of the NAACP, CORE and SCLC effective in meeting the needs of black Americans, up to 1968?

2 'The rise of black radical movements were the direct result of disappointment with the limited gains of peaceful, non-violent protest.' How valid is that view?

3 How successfully did the Civil Rights Movement achieve improvements in the social, economic and political opportunities of black Americans?

4 How important were changes in federal policy to improving the lives of black Americans up to 1968?

Now start planning your conclusion and the first thing to remember is that your essay or extended response **must** have a conclusion. If you do not end with a clearly indicated conclusion you will lose 2 marks. That is a whole results band you would throw away! Your conclusion must do certain things to get the 2 marks and it is not enough just to write a summary of points you have made. The SQA has stated that a good conclusion should be balanced, it should summarise the arguments and it should come to an overall judgement directly related to the question. That is quite a lot to think about when you head towards the end of your extended response and time is likely to be running out, so this top tip is to provide an effective model for a conclusion that can be used in ANY extended response.

Here is the model:

- Sentence/part 1 – 'In conclusion …' – indicates that the conclusion has started. You should suggest there are different points of view about the main idea contained in the question.

- Sentence/part 2 – 'On one hand … ' – provides a summary of some points that take one view of the question.

- Sentence/part 3 – 'On the other hand … ' – completes the summary by summing up the different views and this provides the balance.

- Sentence/part 4 – 'Overall … ' – provides a final answer to the main question, which means you make a decision. You might decide that one idea was more important than the others and that means you are prioritising.

Now apply this to a question such as:

To what extent did the Civil Rights Movement improve the lives of black Americans up until 1968?

In conclusion, the Civil Rights Movement is credited with bringing about the end of racial discrimination in the USA and gaining real civil rights for black Americans; however, some argue the gains were very limited in what they achieved and did little to help large areas of the USA.

On one hand, the campaigns of the NAACP, CORE and SCLC with the leadership of Martin Luther King did help to end segregation and discrimination in the South and persuaded federal government that both a Civil Rights Act and a Voting Rights Act were necessary.

On the other hand, many black Americans, especially those in the black radical groups such as Black Muslims and Black Panthers and supporters of Black Power, argued that the gains in the South did little to help the problems of urban deprivation in American ghettos.

Overall, the Civil Rights Movement did improve the lives of many black Americans in terms of ending segregation and discrimination in the South, but the problems of unemployment, bad housing and poverty were much harder problems to target with marches and sit-ins and so many black Americans still faced problems after 1968. As the Kerner Commission reported, 'America is still two societies, one white and one black, one rich and one poor, separate and unequal.'

It is important that you practise this style of conclusion so you can produce this style under time pressure and without too much hard thinking. After all, it does what you are asked to do. It is balanced, summarises the arguments and it makes an overall judgement so it should be 2 marks guaranteed.

Glossary

Alphabet Agencies – federal departments created to deal with specific features of New Deal policies and referred to/known by their initials.

Anarchist – a word used in America for anyone who threatened to use violence to change the US political system, rather like the way the word terrorist is used today.

Bolshevik – a Russian revolutionary; someone holding revolutionary or politically subversive views.

Brains Trust – a group of expert advisers put together by FDR to suggest ideas to help get America out of the Depression.

Congress – like the UK's Houses of Parliament. It contains the House of Representatives and the Senate

Constitutional Rights – the rights of US citizens guaranteed by the US Constitution.

Double V – a campaign for civil rights launched during World War Two that aimed to achieve victory against America's enemies in the war but also victory for civil rights.

Exports – products made domestically (in the home nation) and sold abroad.

Federal government – the national government of the USA

The Great Migration – the movement of black Americans to the Northern US states between 1914 and 1945.

Imports – products made abroad and brought into the home nation.

Inaugural – a speech given by a new president; also used to mark the beginning of a period of office.

Inferior – less important, less civilised

Isolationism – the belief that America should not become involved in the problems and disputes concerning foreign countries.

Jim Crow laws – a series of laws passed by Southern states following the end of Reconstruction in 1877 continuing through to the mid-1960s, enforcing racial segregation in all areas of life including schools, transport, housing and public spaces. Inter-racial relationships and marriage were also prohibited under Jim Crow rules.

Ku Klux Klan (KKK) – white supremacist, anti-immigration group, first founded in the South following the end of the Civil War but petering out by the close of the century . It enjoyed a resurgence from 1915 onwards, reinventing itself under the slogan "100 per cent Americanism". Its exclusively WASP membership were (are) staunchly opposed to Catholics, Jews, Communists and immigrants as well as their long-standing hatred of African-Americans.

Lynching – the murder of black Americans, usually by mobs of whites, in retaliation for some alleged crime or misdemeanour.

Manifest destiny – the belief of white immigrant settlers in America that all the resources of the USA were provided for them by God and were available to use and develop as they saw fit.

Multi-ethnic – many cultures and races mixed together.

Nativists – old-fashioned Americans who worried that their traditional, small-town American values were under threat from modern society, especially new immigrants.

'New" immigration – after 1880 many more immigrants came from central and eastern Europe and also southern Europe. These were known as 'new' immigrants in contrast to the WASP immigrants of old.

Overproduction – making too much of something so that products remain unsold.

Protectionism – a government policy aimed at protecting domestic industries from foreign competition by using tariffs on imports to make the foreign-made products more expensive than those produced domestically.

Pull reasons – things that attract people to go somewhere in the hope of prosperity and a better life.

Push reasons – things that force people to move to escape difficult situations and hardships.

Rugged Individualism – the belief that individual people should be free to work hard and develop a good life for themselves with minimum government interference just as the original settlers had done.

Saturated market – all likely customers already have the product so no more can be sold.

Segregation – enforced separation of people of different racial groups.

Sharecropping – a system of farming where landowners rent the use of their land to tenant farmers, in return for a share of the crops produced on that section of land.

Shares – people who buy shares are buying a share in a business and when the business makes a profit, shareholders receive a share of the profits. If a business makes a loss the share value falls and shareholders face owning shares worth less than the price they paid for them. Shareholders then have a choice – do they wait for prices to recover of do they sell their shares before the price falls further?

Slavery – the state of one person being 'owned' and exploited by another, usually forced to undertake arduous labour. In the case of the USA, black Africans were captured in West Africa and taken to the USA to be sold. This happened from the early 1550s until the late 1800s, when slavery was abolished.

Subversives – someone who seeks or sets out to undermine or overthrow an established system or institution. Also linked to how we might use the word terrorist in a modern-day context.

Supreme Court – the highest court in the USA. It can overturn decisions made by state and federal courts and decides whether new laws affect the constitutional rights of US citizens.

Tariff – a tax put on certain foreign goods to artificially raise prices within the home nation to encourage citizens to buy domestically produced alternatives, thereby protecting national industries from foreign competition.

Uncle Tom – an insult used against a black American too eager to please white Americans; any African-American who behaved in a subservient way towards white Americans.

Underconsumption – not enough customers for products made

References

Chapter 2

Emma Lazarus *The New Colossus,* (p. 8)

Grace Abbott and Julian W. Mack (1917) *The Immigrant and the Community,* New York: The Century Co. (p. 12)

Speech by Senator Heflin of Alabama, 1921 (p. 12)

Plain Words, anarchist flyer from April 1919 (p. 17)

Chapter 3

The Richmond Times, 12 January 1900 (p. 30)

Booker T. Washington *Atlanta Compromise Speech,* 1895 (p. 39)

Booker T. Washington (16 July 1884) 'The Educational Outlook in the South' reproduced in Louis R. Harlan, ed. (1974) *The Booker T. Washington Papers,* Vol. 2, Urbana: University of Illinois Press, pp. 257–58 (p. 40)

Booker T. Washington (1899) *The Future of the American Negro,* Boston: Small, Maynard & Company (p. 40)

W.E. Burghardt Du Bois (1903) 'Of Mr. Booker T. Washington and Others' (adapted) taken from *The Souls of Black Folk,* Chicago: A.C. McClurg & Co. (p. 41)

Bob Marley *Exodus* © Sony/ATV Music Publishing LLC, Warner/Chappell Music, Inc., Universal Music Publishing Group (p. 42)

Speech given at an NAACP conference in the 1930s (p. 48)

Chapter 4

Alistair Cooke (2009) *Alistair Cooke's America* (New York: Basic Books) (pp. 53 & 69)

New Republic magazine 1932 (p. 60)

John Steinbeck (1939) *The Grapes of Wrath,* Penguin Classics: London (New Ed edition 7 Sept. 2000) original work The Viking Press: New York (p. 61)

New Republic magazine 1933 (p. 67)

Chapter 5

Michael E. Parrish (1994) *Anxious Decades: America in Prosperity and Depression 1920–1941,* New York: W.W. Norton & Company (p. 74)

Inaugural Address of the President, Washington, D.C., 4 March 1933, taken from Franklin D. Roosevelt Library. First Carbon Files 1933–1945 National Archives Identifier: 197333 (https://www.archives.gov/education/lessons/fdr-inaugural/) (p. 76)

Frances Perkins (2011) *The Roosevelt I Knew* (Penguin Classics), New York: Penguin Books (pp. 78 & 85)

Remember my Forgotten Man, LYRICS: AL DUBIN; MUSIC: HARRY WARREN) (1933) featured as finale of Mervin Le Roy's 1933 film "Gold Diggers of 1933" © 1937 M. Witmark & Sons (p. 79)

Herbert Hoover (1953) *The Memoirs of Herbert Hoover Vol. 2 –The Cabinet and the Presidency, 1920–1933,* London: Hollis & Carter (p. 82)

New Republic magazine May 1940 (p. 85)

C. P Hill (1966) *Franklin Roosevelt (The Clarendon biographies)*, London: Oxford University Press (p. 85)

W.E. Leuchtenburg (2009) *Franklin D. Roosevelt and the New Deal: 1932–1940*, New York: Harper Perennial, p. 42 (p. 86 & 88)

Letter sent to President Roosevelt in 1934 (author unknown) (p. 86)

Herbert Hoover (2011) *The Memoirs of Herbert Hoover – The Great Depression, 1929–1941*, Orth Press (original work New York: The Macmillan Company 1952) (p. 86)

C.P. Hill (1967) *The United States since the First World War* (20th Century Histories; No.2), London: George Allen & Unwin p. 59 (pp. 87–88)

William O. Douglas (1948) *Being An American*, New York: John Day (p. 88)

Chapter 6

Big Bill Broonzy *Black Brown and White* composed by Broonzy © Warner/Chappell Music, Inc. (p.94)

John Lewis and Michael D'Orso *Walking with the Wind: A Memoir of the Movement*, New York: Simon & Schuster 2015 (originally published 1998) (p. 95)

Earl Warren, Chief Justice of the U.S. Supreme Court, *Brown v. Board of Education of Topeka*, Opinion; May 17, 1954; Records of the Supreme Court of the United States; Record Group 267; National Archives. (p. 96)

Speech by Martin Luther King, Jnr at the Holt Street Baptist Church during the Montgomery Bus Boycott, 5 December 1955 (p. 100)

President Dwight D. Eisenhower's 1957 Address on Little Rock, Arkansas 'Mob Rule

Cannot Be Allowed to Override the Decisions of Our Courts', 24 September 1957 (p. 102)

Interview with Elizabeth Eckford 1957 (p. 102)

Martin Luther King, Jnr 'Letter from Birmingham Jail' April 1963 (p. 104)

Joseph McNeil quoted in Henry Hampton, Steve Fayer, Sarah Flynn (2011) *Voices Of Freedom: An Oral History of the Civil Rights Movement From the 1950s Through the 1980s*, New York: Random House (p. 105)

James Farmer (1985) *Lay Bare the Heart: An Autobiography of the Civil Rights Movement*, New York: Arbor House (p. 107)

James Lawson 'Eve of Nonviolent Revolution' *Southern Patriot*, 19 (November, 1961) (p. 108)

Martin Luther King, Jnr 'Letter from Birmingham Jail', April 1963 (p. 110)

John F. Kennedy: 'Radio and Television Report to the American People on Civil Rights' 11 June 1963. Online by Gerhard Peters and John T. Woolley, *The American Presidency Project*. http://www.presidency.ucsb.edu/ws/?pid=9271 (p. 112)

Martin Luther King 'Letter from Selma' *The New York Times*, 5 February 1965 (p. 116)

G.B. Leonard 'Journey of Conscience Midnight Plane to Alabama' *The Nation*, 10 May 1965 (p.117)

Martin Luther King, speech at Montgomery, 25 March 1965 (p. 118)

President Lyndon B. Johnson's Special Message to Congress, Sunday 31 March 1968. National Archives and Records Administration, The Lyndon B. Johnson

Library and Museum (http://www.lbjlib. utexas.edu/johnson/archives.hom/speeches. hom/650315.asp) (p. 118)

Martin Luther King, Jnr 'Letter from Birmingham Jail', April 1963 (p. 120)

Chapter 7

Cleveland Sellers (1990) *The River of No Return: The Autobiography of a Black Militant and the Life and Death of SNCC*, Jackson: University Press of Mississippi (p. 129)

Stokely Carmichael 'What We Want' *New York Review of Books* (22nd September 1966) (p. 130)

Stokely Carmichael and Charles Hamilton (1966) *Black Power, New York: Random House* (p. 130)

Lomax, Louis E. 'A Summing Up: Louis Lomax Interviews Malcolm X.' *When the Word Is Given: a Report on Elijah Muhammad, Malcolm X, and the Black Muslim World.* (p. 131)

Malcolm X and George Breitman (1994) *Malcolm X Speaks: Selected Speeches and Statements,* New York: Grove Press (p. 131)

Speech by Malcolm X at the Northern Negro Grass Roots Leadership Conference, 10 November 1963, in King Solomon Baptist Church in Detroit, Michigan (p. 132)

Malcolm X and Alex Haley (1965)*The Autobiography of Malcolm X,* New York: Grove Press (pp. 132–3)

Martin Luther King, Jnr, 'I've Been to the Mountaintop' speech given on 3 April 1968, at the Mason Temple (Church of God in Christ headquarters) in Memphis, Tennessee (p. 136).

United States. Kerner Commission, Report of the National Advisory Commission on Civil Disorders (Washington: U.S. Government Printing Office, 1968) (p. 139)

The Millennium Breach: The American Dilemma, Richer and Poorer: Executive Summary, Milton S. Eisenhower Foundation, 1998 (http://www.eisenhowerfoundation.org/ frames/main_frameMB.html) (p. 140)

Index